Praise for *October Song*

October Song is a beautifully authentic memoir that reminds us that there are no time limits on dreams, creativity is boundless and nothing in life is finite when we let go of our self-imposed rules. By sharing an intimate phase of renewal, Berner reaffirms what we already know, but too often forget ~~th~~ ~~~~ ; just a number when we value the jou~~rn~~ **Michelle Burwell**, *Windy C*~~~~

With his gift of a no-holds ~~~~ ~~~~onest, confessional—Berner succee~~~~ ~~~~, as a master story-teller. Music can tell the story oi our past. Lyrics evoke memories; melodies make the heart thump like it did on a first date. *October Song* brings the reader through a mix tape of life, as Berner tells his tale of new love while traveling through landscapes and time. Each chapter reads like a beloved song.
Geralyn Hesslau Magrady, *Lines*

October Song strikes all the right chords; the high notes and the low notes of a life's journey—the losses, the lessons, the loves. Composed with tenderness and affection, Berner's heartfelt and ultimately life-affirming joyride teaches us that you're never too old to roll down the window, crank it up and belt it out.
Randy Richardson, *Cheeseland: A Novel*

October Song is about and for all who wonder if it's too late to follow a dream. Through his easy conversational tone, David W. Berner shares his heart and soul as if we were curled up together, sipping hot chocolate in front of a fireplace. Like a favorite song, that warm fuzzy feeling lingers on well after the story is done.
Viga Boland, *No Tears for My Father*

David W. Berner takes the reader beyond the mid-life crisis to what comes next: rebirth via newfound passion for music, travel, life and a special someone. *October Song* is a touching story that will inspire anybody of any age searching for meaning in their lives.

Mike O'Mary, *Wise Men and Other Stories*

October Song

A memoir of music and the journey of time

October Song

A memoir of music and the journey of time

David W. Berner

Winchester, UK
Washington, USA

First published by Roundfire Books, 2017
Roundfire Books is an imprint of John Hunt Publishing Ltd., No. 3 East St., Alresford,
Hampshire SO24 9EE, UK
office1@jhpbooks.net
www.johnhuntpublishing.com
www.roundfire-books.com

For distributor details and how to order please visit the 'Ordering' section on our website.

Text copyright: David W. Berner 2016

ISBN: 978 1 78535 556 1
978 1 78535 557 8 (ebook)
Library of Congress Control Number: 2016944525

A CIP catalogue record for this book is available from the British Library.

Design: Stuart Davies

Printed and bound by CPI Group (UK) Ltd, Croydon, CR0 4YY, UK

We operate a distinctive and ethical publishing philosophy in all
areas of our business, from our global network of authors to
production and worldwide distribution.

For the girl in the story

Also by David W. Berner

Accidental Lessons: The Memoir of a Rookie Teacher and a Life Renewed

Any Road Will Take You There: A Journey of Fathers and Sons

There's a Hamster in the Dashboard: A Life in Pets

Night Radio: A Love Story

There's nothing you can do that can't be done.

—The Beatles, "All You Need is Love"

Chapter 1

It was late in the fading light of the first day of the long trip, somewhere on the Tri-State expressway about forty miles southwest of Chicago. With one hand on the steering wheel and the other on my phone, I fiddled with my iTunes playlist, trying to find Dylan's "Subterranean Homesick Blues" in the mess of my music library.

"Relax, babe," I said, smiling.

"How'd you think I'd feel about you if you killed us," Leslie grumbled, more nervous than upset.

The car had swerved a bit but I'd stayed in my lane. Leslie insisted I'd been trying to text someone, probably my son, but I'm pretty sure I was looking for that song, one of Dylan's most lyrically creative tracks, the one with the snappy rhymes and the jazzlike, stream of consciousness lyrics. It's been said that Dylan was probably inspired to write the song after reading *The Subterraneans*, Jack Kerouac's novel. That may not have been true, but I liked that kind of artistic association, so I was going with the story.

"It'll be all right," I said.

"Relax, babe? Really?" Leslie laughed. "Not exactly relaxed when you're all over the road."

"Okay, okay," I said. "I guess it wouldn't be good to die before we get started."

"Let's at least get a few hours in before you endanger our lives," she said.

I put my phone in the cup holder between the seats and touched her leg.

"I am so happy you're here." Keeping my eyes on the highway, I kissed the tips of the index and middle fingers of my right hand and planted them on her cheek.

"Me, too," she said. "It's so cool."

Two month ago, I entered a songwriting contest. It was a complete whim. I had set up a Google alert on my computer for anything connected to writing or writers, as I had published a couple of books, and every morning I was emailed a list of articles or blog entries connected somehow to those two subjects. One morning the alert sent me a Web announcement for Rapunzel's 12th Annual Songwriting Contest. Now, I play guitar. I've written some songs, mostly for the fun of it, nothing serious, although I take the writing seriously. I put my heart into it, but I'd never sold a song or professionally recorded one. But you know how this goes: everyone who has ever played guitar has dreamed of being a rock star.

I used to play in a band in my early twenties and performed at some coffeehouses and bars with another guitarist. Rich was more of a lead guy; I was more rhythm and picked a little. We liked the same music—Dylan, Stephen Stills, The Eagles. I'm sorry now to say we even played some America. The lead singer, Dewey Bunnell, sounded like a less-harsh Neil Young, and the band's debut album was pretty damn good. They turned lame and sappy after that, but hey, America was big at the time. Our band got pretty good, too, but of course we were never going to be stars. Hell, we were happy to get a gig at a dive saloon on a Friday night. The songs I wrote back then were folky, the same kind of material I wrote in college. The benefit to those kinds of songs, at least back then, was that the songs sometimes impressed girls. In the two or three years after the undergraduate years, I wrote maybe one or two others. They were nearly always about where I was in my life at the time, personal songs about a relationship I was in or about to end. When I look back at those years now, writing those songs was like writing entries in a diary.

It was thirty years until I wrote another song.

Marriage, kids, Little League practice, and my career as a reporter took priority over any silly rock 'n' roll dream. The Fillmore East would have to wait. The Rock and Roll Hall of

Fame would have to wait. I had a bathroom to paint, a yard to mow, and kids to pick up at school.

Then, after a divorce and a career shift from daily reporter to teaching college, I found myself in Florida, writing at Jack Kerouac's house in Orlando.

I was a lucky guy. Somehow, the members of the board of the Jack Kerouac Project liked the personal story I sent them about a brief and unexpected encounter with Muhammad Ali at Chicago's O'Hare airport. The story was about how my father's dream of being a boxer had shown up in the DNA of my children, especially my youngest, Graham. From the time he was ten until he was about seventeen, Graham wanted to fight. When my father was a teenager, he boxed with his school buddies in the basement of his parents' house. Graham watched a lot of boxing and mixed-martial arts on TV. My dad had shown him the traditional boxer's stance, where to keep his fists, how to punch. And then, coming down the corridor at Terminal One at O'Hare one morning while waiting for a flight for a getaway to Oregon with my kids, there was Muhammad Ali. There's poetry in that. So, I wrote about it. It all fit together somehow. And the board of the Kerouac Project thought so, too. So much so that they awarded me a writer-in-residence opportunity, a chance to write for a couple of summer months in Kerouac's home, an old tin roof Florida cottage where he pounded out *The Dharma Bums* on a manual typewriter late into the night. During my time there, I worked on a manuscript of my own but also wrote a few songs, the first attempt in decades. Kerouac's humble little house was such an inspirational place; it had such an artistic vibe emanating from its walls. It coaxed me to pick up the guitar and compose again. I also was at the end of a relationship with a woman back in Chicago. That gave me some material for at least one song. I wrote another about a cross-country road trip I had taken. All road songs are good ones, right? But the one I thought really stood out was the third one, a song about my two sons. They were teenagers at the time: one in high school, the other in college. I won't get into all the details, but they had been struggling with school, finding their own way, some health matters, life stuff. And while they wrestled with it all, I was some 1500 miles away in the middle of Florida. I thought "A Better Day" had a nice rhythm and positive, relatable lyrics. And it seemed perfect for Rapunzel's competition.

A few years later, back home in Chicago, I wrote another song, a love song. It was for Leslie. We had been together about three months when I composed "Under the Moon." I was compelled to write it, the same way I was compelled to write the one for my boys. At that time, my sons had not yet heard "A Better Day." They would have felt ridiculously self-conscious if I played it for them. But the song for Leslie, well, I had to sing that one to her in person. I'll admit, I was nervous; worried I might be opening up my heart too much too soon. But she didn't run or hide when I strummed the guitar and sang the lyrics to her for the first time. That was a good sign. I hadn't looked into the eyes of a woman and sung a song like that in a very long time.

"Who does this kind of thing?" Leslie asked, after I played. I sensed she might have been a little overcome by the gesture, this old guy with the diminished singing range, picking his way through minor and major chords.

"I guess I'm not a guy who hides his feelings," I said. "That can be either wonderful or a complete disaster."

She kissed me and appeared as if she were holding back tears. Chalk one up for the romantics in the world.

So, there I was with two decent songs. One fresher than the other, but in both cases I believed I'd put together a pretty good combination of words and music. No Lennon and McCartney stuff, but not bad. Plus, I had already made MP3 files of each, crudely recording the songs using a Radio Shack microphone and a little mini recorder and stored them on my computer. Nothing special. It was just a way to have a record of the music, a lazy way to compose, really, so I didn't have to transpose the music with chords or scales.

I attached the music files to an email addressed to Rapunzel's and hit SEND.

I hadn't thought it through much. It was just some silly contest and what was Rapunzel's anyway? Maybe just some shabby bar in a remote part of Virginia and maybe this contest was nothing more than an Appalachian version of *The Gong Show*, that 1970s TV program that mocked awful amateur performers. After sending the email with the songs, I forgot about the competition.

Three weeks later, I received a response.

"I'm a finalist. One of my songs made the cut," I told Leslie over the phone. I was perplexed, somewhat astonished, and skeptical. *This contest must be nothing, just some crappy, regional thing put together to spike beer sales at the dive that was Rapunzel's. And who really would pick one of my songs? Really? There must be a hundred applicants who were a lot more talented than me?*

"There are thirty finalists, and all of them—including me—are being asked to come to Virginia to perform live," I added.

This was ridiculous. Nuts. *What was I going to do? Travel some 700 miles to play a three-minute song in front of a bunch of drunks in a bar?*

"You have to do this!" Leslie said, without hesitation. "You simply *have* to go."

"I don't know."

"You're going," she insisted.

"I think I need to find out more about this place, the contest, and everything," I said, continuing with my doubts. "It just seems a little crazy."

I sounded like a sad, old man. In my twenties, I would never have questioned traveling there and performing my song. I would have driven to Peru to sing music I had written. But at fifty-seven, I was wary, cautious. *Could I get time off from my freelance reporting work at CBS Radio in Chicago, and a day or two from the college where I taught? What would it cost? Is this worth it? Why should I do this? This is stupid.*

But just as I was questioning the idea, I was also thinking about whether my guitar needed new strings and how to best work in some practice. One of the songs, the one about the boys, I hadn't sung in years. Still, I could pull it together with some concentrated effort, right? Hell, I used to do this all the time. I'd memorize chords, licks, and lyrics every week for all those gigs decades ago. Hemingway wrote in *A Farewell to Arms*: "Old men don't grow wise. They grow careful." I did not feel old, and certainly did not want to be careful.

I got on the Internet.

I googled Rapunzel's. I googled Lovingston, Virginia, Rapunzel's hometown. I googled the Blue Ridge Mountains. I googled music in western Virginia. I googled famous songwriting contests. I watched YouTube videos. And I found enough to make up my mind.

The area around Charlottesville, Virginia, just north of Lovingston and Rapunzel's has been a hub of indie musicians for years. The Dave Matthews Band is from Charlottesville. They got their start in the region. Maybe they even played at Rapunzel's in the early going, who knows. Guitar players, fiddlers, harmonica and mandolin players have flocked to central Virginia to play in music-lover bars, taverns, and on stages big and small. One might describe the area as a mini Nashville, at least the way Nashville once was when it was still friendly to songwriters. Rapunzel's was said to be a welcoming place for musicians. Plus, it appeared relatively famous. It not only had local wines, local beers, even espresso, and shelves littered with secondhand books, but it also had an elevated stage, a solid sound system, and an honest-to-goodness professional recording studio. Like the Empty Bottle in Chicago, maybe even The Troubadour in Los Angeles, Rapunzel's was the spot for new, emerging, evolving artists; a folky, alternative country mecca in a small town just east of the Blue Ridge Mountains, in the heart of Virginia's wine country; a big red barn of a building, dusty and funky and rough around the edges, and absolutely, superbly magnificent.

"It looks pretty legitimate," I explained to Leslie. "Rapunzel's has some weight in the music community, it seems."

"So then, you are going?" she asked.

I suddenly felt so very young, the way I did when Rich, my old guitar friend, and I were booked to play our first gig at a coffeehouse on the campus of Clarion State College in Pennsylvania; young like I did when my college girlfriend agreed to drive with me to Florida over winter break; young like I did when I wrote one of my first songs in a cabin in Cook Forest in the Allegheny Mountains during a weekend getaway with college friends, a song I was proud of even though it was an annoying, entirely corny, John Denver-esque ode to the wilderness.

"Would you go with me?" I asked.

"I most definitely would go with you!" Leslie said.

That did it.

Still, there was one thing I needed to tell Leslie before any details could be worked out on whether to fly or drive, when we'd leave, or how long we'd stay.

"Good news and bad news," I said. "The good news is I'm a finalist, of course. I told you that. The bad news . . ." I paused. "They didn't pick your song."

Leslie laughed. "What's with that?"

It didn't matter. She was still going and so was I.

We had five hours of driving before we'd reach the first night's hotel, a Holiday Inn Express in Washington Courthouse, Ohio, a town I didn't even know existed until I mapped out the two-day route to Lovingston. It would be our first hotel of a five-day trip that would include endless driving through mountain towns, lots of wine, startling scenery, and more than two dozen original songs, one performed by a middle-aged guy with an old Yamaha six string resting on his knee, and his best girl cheering him on from the front row.

* * *

It was late when we pulled off to a rest stop somewhere in Indiana, just past the towering and eerily futuristic wind farms in the dreadfully flat terrain near Chalmers. As I waited for Leslie to return to the car, I caught my reflection in the rearview mirror. *Who the hell is that guy?* Time had so altered what I was seeing and so changed the man who was looking back. In that moment alone in the parking lot in the cool darkness of a late October evening, I detected echoes from so many years ago. There before me was the image of a young man with wavy, shoulder-length brown hair, and wire-rimmed glasses like John Lennon wore, checking himself out in the car's mirror just before heading into a neighborhood tavern and a stool near the bar to play America's "Horse With No Name" and maybe a melody of his own, something he wrote late one Saturday night in his dorm room. All he had to do was find the courage to share it with the beer-drinking crowd, who, although barely half-listening, was secretly longing to hear something special.

Chapter 2

There were salty tears in the corners of my eyes.

"Girl from the North Country"—Dylan's song of longing and past love—appeared in the random playlist on my iTunes library and quietly played from my car's speakers as we traveled somewhere along the gloomily flat terrain near the border of Indiana and Ohio. I had a lot of Dylan in my playlist.

"What the hell is it with me?" I asked, not expecting an answer. We were getting closer to Dayton now. We'd missed an exit and had to circle back to point the car toward I-70. I had spilled gasoline on my sweatpants—my comfortable driving uniform—when I carelessly overfilled the tank somewhere near Indianapolis. I had to change into jeans, the pair I had planned to wear for the performance. The little Nissan had no traditional trunk, so I tossed the saturated sweatpants on the floor in the backseat and for a hundred miles, the vaporous odor assaulted the inside of the car.

"You're just clumsy," Leslie answered, jokingly.

"It's not that. Not the pants," I said.

"I'm confused. Are the pants making you high?"

I laughed.

"No, it's the damn song," I said, turning up the volume a bit.

Leslie listened.

"It's just *you*. It's who you are," she said.

"I'm not sad. I don't long for some girl 'from the north country.' But songs like this make me cry all the freakin' time," I said.

Leslie reached for my hand and laced her fingers in mine.

Joni Mitchell's "A Case of You." Ray LaMontagne's "Jolene." Graham Nash's "Sleep Song." Dozens of others. Songs of yearning. I find myself singing the words and quietly crying. Not bawling, just a little whimpering. I'm not lovesick. I'm not longing for something. It's just the echoes, those cruel echoes of the past, past loves, people now gone from a life. Every love has left a mark, all the way back to middle school. I too am left with tenderness, like the inky sting of a tattoo artist's needle when he is done. It started in middle school. Her name was Michelle. Dark, shoulder-length hair, the walk of a ballerina, toes pointed outward, always a straight back. Michelle had good posture. She was quick to laugh. And if a seventh grader is truly able to exude elegance, she could. She sent me notes in class. Her friends told me she "liked" me, and I was her puppy love slave. But it wasn't actually Michelle that turned me to mush. It was the *idea* of Michelle.

Elton John's "Madman Across the Water" now played from the car's speakers.

"Now there's a song I don't remember ever tearing up over," I said. "'Tiny Dancer' maybe, but not 'Madman.'"

Leslie looked out of the passenger window. "You'd tear up at 'Jingle Bells.'"

"Harsh!" I laughed, and changed the subject. "How far?"

Leslie looked at the map on her phone. "It's a ways to . . . what is it again? Washington Court House?"

"Strange name for a town," I said. "Can you keep going a little longer with that smell?"

"I kind of like it," Leslie said, her eyes still focused out the window and on the lights in houses in the distance. "Reminds me of motorboats, the ones all around when I went to Wisconsin on vacation as a kid."

"What if I snore tonight?" I grinned.

"I brought swimmer's earplugs," Leslie laughed.

"Geez, I'm that bad?"

"Just being prepared, baby."

Leslie tightened the grip around my fingers and pulled my hand closer to relax it on her leg. With my other on the steering wheel's remote audio controls, I lowered the volume of Elton

John's song of loneliness and mistaken madness to allow the whir of the wheels to overtake the music and fill the car's compartment.

I never wondered why lovely Michelle from middle school liked me. Not that I was an overly confident kid or anything, I just figured this is how things went. Girls reached out to boys that made them laugh and didn't look too hideous. I could tell a stupid joke pretty well, and I looked okay. I had a mop top, a Beatles-esque haircut with bangs swooping across my forehead. I wasn't awkwardly shy and I made friends pretty easily. I remember our first kiss. It came behind the west wall of the school. It was a Friday afternoon after classes had let out and I was waiting for my bus. No one could see us. It was just a peck as innocent as a Disney movie. We hung out with friends at her house on the weekends, gathering on the big side porch, and listening to albums by The Grass Roots on her portable record player, "I'd Wait a Million Years" blaring out of little speakers. Michelle and I kissed a lot more over the next two years, groped a bit, both of us terribly self-conscious about it. But we were a couple. Classmates recognized us. We went to school dances together, she wore a dime-store ring, I attended her dance club performances and she came to see me in school plays. Then, unexpectedly, her parents insisted we split. Michelle left a note inside my locker, a neatly folded handwritten goodbye letter with a small red heart drawn on the outside.

In many ways, Michelle—or the idea of Michelle—has shaped every relationship I've had since then, sometimes in a big way and other times small. Whatever that was—love, infatuation, innocent desire—it still rises from my memory like it was yesterday. But every woman I have loved since still tugs at the strings Michelle left hanging from my heart. The ashes of that long-ago relationship, those remnants, permanently settled in a deep corner of me and jump up into view like the heads in the Whac-A-Mole game. All I need is a good song to set me off.

* * *

Washington Court House, Ohio, is a town of about 14,000 people, a suburb of Columbus. It is said to have a number of historic buildings, some of them on the National Register. The town's website promotes the downtown as cute and quaint, like hundreds of other towns. There was a story on the site about how the place had an unusual pattern of streets. All of the town's roads ran northeast–southwest and northwest–southeast instead of the typical north–south and east–west. The founders apparently set it up like this so the big white county courthouse would be in sunlight every moment of the day. Sunlight was long gone when we drove off the highway. It was somewhere around 9:30 at night, and the exit off Route 35 that would have led us to downtown Washington Court House was midnight black. If I remember correctly, all we could see just off the highway was a big store—maybe a K-Mart or Wal-Mart—a gas station, our hotel—the Holiday Inn Express—and a place called Dakota's Roadhouse, a chain restaurant. A few cars were parked outside, but not enough to prove the place was open.

"Aw, Dakota's," Leslie sighed. Dakota was the name of her Labrador-Chow mix.

"This looks like our only option in the big metropolis," I said. We were hungry and I hoped Dakota's was still serving. At this point anything but McDonald's would have done the trick. Fast food felt like the wrong choice to end the night. Greasy, salty, heavy. Not good.

I stepped from the car and walked to the door while Leslie waited. If the restaurant wasn't open, it would be Lay's potato chips and AriZona Ice Tea from the gas station. Dakota's door was hard and heavy, made of solid wood. It didn't squeak when it opened, it growled.

"You serving food?" I asked the hostess behind the takeout counter, a girl who looked too young to be in high school.

"Yep, still open. Food until midnight," she said, flashing a cheerleader grin.

I gave her one of those silly thumbs-up gestures, something your not-so-cool uncle might do.

"Good to go," I said to Leslie, sliding into the driver's seat. I parked the car and hung the still stinky, gasoline-soaked pair of sweatpants on the outside rearview mirror.

"You don't think someone will steal them?" Leslie asked.

"Gasoline pants in the middle of bum-fuck Ohio?"

Dakota's had some sort of theme going, but I'm just not sure exactly what it was. It seemed an odd mix of Western, cowboy, rustic farmhouse, and sports bar. In the entranceway was a nearly life-sized, black-and-white photograph of John Wayne dressed in chaps, vest, and Stetson hat, a publicity shot from an old movie. On the opposite wall were drawings and photos of Wild Bill Hickok and Annie Oakley. When we followed the hostess to our table, I saw a huge banner for the Cincinnati Bengals hanging over the bar, and on the wall next to the beer taps was a neonlike electric sign with an orange flashing Bengals' helmet appearing to hang from the *R* in Budweiser.

"Bengals' country?" I asked the twenty-something waiter, knowing the answer.

"Yeah, they're a big deal around here," he said, handing us menus. "I'm from Texas, so, whatever."

"Steelers' fan," I whispered.

"Don't matter to me," he replied, with his slow drawl. "But it does get a little crowded in here on Sunday. A lot of orange."

I ordered a beer. Leslie asked for a big glass of water. Behind her and to my right, a few booths over her shoulder, I could see two men in their fifties, about my age—gray haired, balding, and beer bellied—slopping down mugs of beer, each with an empty glass next to him, leftover suds sliding down their insides. I hadn't missed their expressions when the two guys slowly watched Leslie walk by as the hostess seated us, their eyes following her like some lusty synchronized optical exam. And now one of them was ogling her again. I caught his eye and locked in. He quickly diverted his stare, knocked back a few big swallows, pretending he'd really been watching the TV over the bar.

I had never fought over a girl before. Not to say I wouldn't have, or hadn't thought about it sometime or another when I was young and stupid. Can't say jealousy has never overwhelmed me. In fact, there had been times when another guy eyes-up your girl and all you want to do is gloat. Still, there were times in my younger days when I may have wanted to pop some idiot who flirted with my date or said something lewd to a girl at a party, but I was too chicken to actually do it. And I wasn't going to start something now, of course. Still, I must admit—right then and there—I might have clocked the guy if he had kept it up.

"Goofy hicks around here," I muttered under my breath.

"What was that?" Leslie asked.

"Nothing."

It was a terribly ignorant remark, really. I immediately felt bad for thinking it, and worse for saying it, even if no one heard. What did I have against these guys? They were just trying to have a couple of beers on a Friday night. They saw a good-looking lady walk by and they acknowledged it. I might have done the same thing.

"Just watching the table behind you," I said.

Leslie began to turn around.

"No, don't," I said. "No big deal. Forget it."

Leslie's eyes zeroed in on mine and lingered. A slow smile emerged. I think she knew exactly what I had been thinking.

I had a second beer and a chicken sandwich. Leslie, who buys unpasteurized wheatgrass juice and makes a killer kale dish with onions and garlic, uncharacteristically loaded up on a plate of nachos. The anticipation of the trip had fueled us for 350 miles, but now we were full and tired and the Holiday Inn was just down the street. The night's coolness had helped air out the gasoline pants. They smelled far better. I tossed them on the car's rear seat for the night, and we carried only the bags we needed into the hotel, along with my guitar. Someone breaking into the car and stealing the old six string seemed highly unlikely, but I wasn't taking that chance, no matter the odds, not now. Within minutes we were under the covers in the king-sized bed, Leslie's bare legs entangled in mine, the swimmer's plugs in her ears.

In the early morning, I awoke to see slivers of dim sunlight edging through the folds in the curtains. Leslie was still sleeping—a peaceful, silent rest. I tossed a few times, hoping to catch another few minutes, but my mind was racing. I stared at the ceiling and sang the lyrics to "A Better Day" silently in my head. I'd practiced but maybe not enough, and recalling song lyrics, something that was so easy years ago, was harder now, almost laborious. Plus, somewhat oddly, I still had those two men on my mind, the ones who had been eyeing Leslie at the bar the night before. Eight hours later, I was feeling like a dopey schoolboy about it all. I was physically rested but emotionally restless. I was trying to remember the song and forget those guys, and at the same time, trying to figure out how to balance the feelings I had about where I'd been and where I was going. I was at a crossroads, as cliché as that sounds. But it was true. There had been times in my life when I had believed I was shadow-boxing, throwing punches at myself, swinging at portions of my past. The songwriting contest and this trip had forced some of those old feelings to resurface, to remember the gigs and the music and the songs from decades before. And now I could add the reawakened emotions of an adolescent. I hated when I found out that Michelle, the high-school girlfriend, had moved on and was dating someone new. It wasn't jealousy; it was a sense of loss. And it was loss again when the seven-year relationship with my college girlfriend was over, and more loss when my marriage ended. And now here I was, a middle-aged man, carrying old scars and at the same time singing a new song. I was lying in bed with a wonderful woman whom I'd found magically matched my spirit, yet I was wrestling with past losses and the fear of new ones, bouncing between the old me and new me. Shadowboxing again. Like before, I could see the boxer's silhouette on the wall, and it was mine. I was swinging at myself, the shadow of a lovesick schoolboy and a heartbroken man who at times believed he could change the world, be someone special, an international reporter, a great, big important, influential grownup, be a rock star. Instead, he had discovered he was simply *normal*, and struggling, like everyone else, with love and lust and finding my authentic self. I grew up to find a good job in broadcasting, got married, bought a four-bedroom colonial, raised two boys, played golf on the weekends, and fell into the soft, comfortable suburban life. It was wonderful. It really was. But the foundation of the house I had built was uneven, my core buried under concrete basement blocks. I'm certain the entombment had partly contributed to the failure of my marriage, and afterward it added to a list of uncertainties as I stumbled through a series of relationships. And through them all I had remained that shadow boxer, swinging away at the dark outlines of a ghost, someone I thought I was. And now, in the early morning of small-town Ohio, there was again evidence of that past, shadows lingering. But there was also hard proof of change. I was on the edge of a new place, a new road, heading in a new destination, and now alone with my thoughts, despite my frenetic mind, the attempt to remember the words of my song, and those old, familiar silhouettes on the wall, I believed, maybe, I was no longer compelled to box the old me. I think it was David Bowie who said something about how aging is such an extraordinary thing—it permits us to grow into who we are really supposed to be.

Leslie—tight inside the sheets—opened her eyes, took out an earplug, and snuggled close.

"Good morning, you," I whispered, from my side of the bed.

"Hi, you," she said, in a sleepy voice.

"You heard me with those in?" I asked.

She smiled and said, "Just enough."

We drank bad hotel coffee, ate fake scrambled eggs, and were on the road again by 7:30, a half-day away from Virginia.

Chapter 3

A week before leaving Chicago, I bought a new set of guitar strings—Martin, medium gauge. I love new strings. They have this unmistakable clean, sinewy snap when you play them for the first time. It's a perfect sound. But I don't like stringing a new set; my guitar is over forty years old, some of the tuners have become tricky to adjust, one is stripped, and a bridge pin that holds in the knobby end of the D string doesn't fit as tightly anymore. Stringing up the old Yamaha GF-160 these days is like running a mile. I can do it, but it takes way longer than it used to and not all my parts hold up so well.

The competition was now twelve hours away. I figured I still had time to put on the new strings.

"I can't believe you're doing this with me," I said to Leslie, as we walked to the car.

"Wouldn't want to be anywhere else," she said.

When Leslie smiles, she has this delicious crinkle in her nose and her eyes illuminate like the bulbs on a child's Christmas tree.

"Who else in the world would agree to do this with me?" I said, searching for the car keys in my pocket.

After double-checking Google Maps, I snaked the car out of the parking lot, an awkward design that made it difficult to understand where to find the exit and the road that would lead us to the highway. We were some 400 miles away from the next hotel. After that, it would then be another half an hour of driving to Lovingston and Rapunzel's. But we also wanted to allow some time to explore. Central Virginia is loaded with wineries. Not something we expected. When I first received word of the finalist designation, I thought we might be heading into Appalachia and a weekend that would remind me of a scene from the movie *Deliverance*. But after Leslie googled all matters of central Virginia, she found the area had a foodie culture and lots of wine, dating back to Thomas Jefferson's time. Monticello, Jefferson's home, wasn't far from where we were headed. Not just dozens of wineries, but hundreds. Who knew? Although this fact was a surprise, the natural beauty was even more so. Not just in Virginia, either. The mountains and gorges and bluffs through West Virginia had stunned us. I grew up in Pittsburgh, an hour from West Virginia, and thought I knew the state. I camped there a couple of times when I was in my early twenties, skied there too. But I had not traveled where we were, near the Ohio border. We passed Chillicothe and Jackson then over the Ohio River into the Mountain State.

"Okay, things are changing," I said, pulling the car into a gas station somewhere near the border town of Point Pleasant, West Virginia.

"A lot more hills. Mountains," said Leslie.

"Not just that," I said, pointing to a sign above the door next to the service station's entrance.

BISCUIT WORLD.

"We're in the south now," Leslie said.

This place sells the kind of food your doctor tells you not to eat. Biscuits and gravy are at the top of the menu board. You can get your order with sausage, eggs, and bacon or all three at once, heaped on top, and with a separate side order of bacon. You cross a river, turn a corner, and suddenly the culture makes a wide shift. We were now right in the middle of the world of buttermilk biscuits.

From the Ohio River all the way to Charleston, the state capitol, I'd bet we saw a dozen signs for Biscuit World restaurants.

"Heart attack on a plate," I said, after seeing yet another Biscuit World sign along Route 35. I knew a little something about a heart attack.

It had been some eighteen months since I crawled into Rush Hospital outside of Chicago early on a Friday morning feeling as if someone were sitting on my chest.

"There's pressure, lots of it," I told the nurse at the emergency room reception desk.

I had experienced some discomfort the day before. It wasn't pain, instead it was like congestion in the chest, like something one gets with a bad cold. I tried medicating with some over-the-counter remedies, but the next morning, the pressure was still there. I was scheduled to work for the radio station that day, the CBS all-news station where I occasionally did freelance reporting. I believed I could tough it out, so I headed up to Chicago's Northwest Side to cover a series of recent neighborhood muggings. However, as I tried to interview neighbors living on the two blocks where the crimes had happened, my chest became achingly heavy and I couldn't stand up straight without pain. My breathing was labored. I knew now it was more than a cold, but didn't want to admit what I somehow instinctively believed. I called my editor, told him I was sick, and drove myself to the hospital. Not the one closest to where I was reporting, but the one nearest to my home, some ten miles away. Stupid. I foolishly was thinking about convenience, not life or death. The traffic was heavy.

When I arrived, a nurse immediately walked me inside a curtained-off area in the emergency room. Doctors and technicians quickly came in and out, checking my pulse, listening to my chest, asking questions, hooking me up to machines that pulsed and flashed.

"We think you might be having a heart attack," the young female doctor said, while holding a clipboard and jotting something down. "We're not sure yet, so we've called in a cardiologist."

Oddly, I wasn't stunned or even worried. Somehow, I already believed it was the heart, and I certainly knew I was in the right place.

As they wheeled me down the hallway to an operating room,

I tried to call my son Graham on my cellphone. No answer. I didn't want to leave a message. I then tried my girlfriend.

"Hey," she said. Her name was Tori. She and I had been together off and on for two years and had tried hard to make it work, but ultimately there would be too many fits and starts. In a couple of months it would all be over. But at that moment, I needed her and she needed me.

"I only have a moment. But I just wanted you to know I think I had a heart attack and they're taking me in to fix it right now."

Silence.

"I'm okay, really. But could you call Graham and let him know." My older son Casey was at college, hundreds of miles away. I didn't want to worry him. Graham lived with his mother a few miles west of the hospital.

"Where are you?" she asked calmly. Tori was good at calm.

I had to think about that question for a moment. "Ah, where am I? Ah, oh, Rush Hospital. Rush in Oak Park. I got to hang up now. Okay?"

"I love you," she said.

"I love you, too."

Despite our difficulties, we still cared.

There was a minor blockage in a small artery. Doctors threaded a long thin tube from a vein on the inside of my thigh all the way to my heart and broke apart the logjam. I was semiconscious through it all and groggily watched the procedure on a monitor above my bed. It took less than an hour.

Not long afterward, Graham arrived at the hospital.

"You trying to scare the shit of out of me?" he asked. Graham was clearly shaken. I tried to be strong.

"Buddy! How are you?" I asked, unsuccessfully trying to divert attention.

"What are you trying to do to me?" Graham asked, putting his arms around my shoulder.

I assured him I was okay. The doctors said I would be fine, no restrictions, and there was no damage.

Tori made it to the hospital shortly after. She crawled into bed with me, holding me for a long time. The nurse never questioned it.

I was home in three days, and two weeks later, I was in the cardiologist's office for a follow-up.

"You did what?" the doctor asked.

"I took my bike out. Did about twelve miles," I said.

He leaned back in his chair and paused, then said, "You felt nothing. No pain."

"A little nauseous, but it went away pretty fast."

I was lucky.

"I see here your father had a heart attack," the doctor said. He looked up from his notes. "Same age."

I smiled.

"DNA. The genes. Hard to fight that," the doctor added.

My father's heart attack forced a bypass operation, months of recovery, and doctor's orders to consider retirement. He, too, was lucky. But Dad was never the same afterward; the attack smothered the vigor that had partially defined him. He now knew, for the first time in his life, he was no longer immortal. He no longer stood as straight; his firm handshake no longer as certain.

The doctor and I went over my diet, my exercise, and I made another appointment.

"Be well," the doctor said. "And it's okay to have a steak now and then, just not every day." He patted me on the back. "You turned a big corner, young man."

At first I didn't know exactly what he meant by "turned a big corner." Sure, there was the obvious. I got through a health crisis, possibly even dodged death, and making it to the hospital before things worsened certainly made a difference in my recovery time. But what was the *corner*? Did getting through this mean I had a new lease on life? But, what kind of life? Did it mean I had learned a lesson about taking care of myself, even though I didn't believe I was some kind of slug? Or did it simply mean that I had reached a fork in the road and for whatever reason was lucky enough to have traveled along the right path, the one that kept me alive?

I read in a book once, can't remember which one or the author, but it was a memoir about a woman who spent her youth riding and showing horses. Her coach had told her in the early years of training how important corners were. He insisted that the corners in a horse arena were where things happened. At those corners, the animal has to swiftly and expertly move its hind legs under its muscular body, keep its balance, steady its speed, and move in a completely different direction without tumbling. And it's where the rider must skillfully assist the horse, allowing the beast to do what is natural, yet guiding it through a smooth and steady turn.

Even if I hadn't had the heart attack, I probably still wouldn't have stopped for a plate of biscuits and gravy in West Virginia. But if I really had wanted to I could have. I could do anything now, it seemed.

* * *

Charleston, West Virginia, appeared to rise out of the mountains. Although it sits in a valley where the Elk and Kanawha Rivers meet, it felt as if it was born out of the hills. It is Daniel Boone country. Coal country. It's the state capitol, the largest city in the state, but it somehow appeared to be pretending to be something it wasn't. I probably had no right to make that assumption. All we did is drive through. But first impressions are first impressions.

"Wonder what people do in Charleston?" I asked, as we made our way over one of the many bridges. The golden-domed capitol building emerged out of the autumn colors.

"Pretty," Leslie said.

"Some university is here, I think."

"All the government work, too."

I grew up in western Pennsylvania and went to college in the middle of the state. I had traveled. I had seen Florida, California, Georgia, North Carolina, Washington State, Oregon, Utah, Michigan, Wisconsin, Texas, Vermont, and Maine. I had been to London and Dublin. I had visited Scotland, France, the Dominican Republic, and Canada. I wouldn't say I was worldly, but I had been around. Still, Charleston was so different from all those places. Every village, city, neighborhood has its unique character, its worth, its stand-alone oneness. Charleston stood out.

"Towns are like people," I said, with the city in the rearview mirror.

"Is that another Biscuit World?" Leslie asked, eyeing a sign near a series of buildings on the eastern edge of Charleston.

"And then they're all the same, too, aren't they?" I laughed.

Some twenty miles outside Charleston, near a small village called Cabin Creek, we stopped to use the bathrooms and get coffee.

"There's a McDonald's," I said. "Best we're going to do." Just like miles ago in Washington Court, Ohio, neither of us had the stomach for fast-food burgers, but our bladders were screaming for a place to pee.

The highway ran along the Kanawha River. Train cars loaded with coal sat on the tracks near its banks. I could just see the arches mix with the taller, older industrial buildings adjacent to it. The highway exit turned tight against the river and the steep hills on the north side of the road. The closer we drove, the more the McDonald's appeared out of place, as if it were an intrusion of lazy, modern convenience, plopped down in an empty lot, swept clean of coal dust. Inside, several old men dressed in overalls and dirty caps, bearded and big bellied, sat together around a yellow table near a window, laughing through what northerners might call hillbilly accents. Each appeared as if just that morning, one by one, they had walked out of a deep West Virginia mine, washed their hands with lye soap, threw cool water on their faces, and handed in their retirement papers.

Many years ago, when I was a young man, fresh out of college, I worked at a radio station in Pittsburgh. Across the street from the downtown studios was an old carryout restaurant. Chipped Formica tables and metal swivel chairs were bolted down in rows. Above the chest-high counter was a menu fashioned with magnetic black letters so they could be adjusted and changed as the menu changed. But the menu never changed, and some of the letters had remained cockeyed or missing for years. Rotisserie chicken spun in a glass case. The place smelled of grease. And at eight o'clock every morning, around a table near the window that looked out toward Sixth Avenue near the north end of downtown, three tired, gray-haired men sat with Styrofoam cups of black coffee. Their faces blank, emotionless. Sometimes they had something to say to each other; most of the time they didn't. And later in the morning, I'd see them again through the window, still sitting, still drinking coffee. Then hours later, after I had run down from the studio to buy a midday cup, there they remained, sipping silently.

"That's going to be us, you know?" said my radio colleague. He was a college buddy who came to work at the station a short time after me, and started joining me for the coffee breaks. We were twenty-five years old.

"That's fucking sad, man," I said.

"You and me, lingering over shitty coffee, talking about Social Security and our doctor's appointments."

During the year or so we had worked together, my friend and I never sat inside the restaurant and drank our coffees. We always took them to go.

The men in that coal country McDonald's reminded me of the men in the timeworn steel town carryout, men who appeared tired and sad to the rest of the world but somehow knew the secret of contentment—the daily predictability of black coffee and old friends.

* * *

The midday views from the car were like murals, the season's earth tones littering the mountains and reaching into the blue sky a few miles east of Charleston.

"This is stunning," whispered Leslie, as if all of it had taken her by surprise. "Amazing country."

"Somewhere around here is White Sulphur Springs," I said. "That's where The Greenbrier is, that big old resort."

The Greenbrier is a stately place. Sam Snead was once the golf pro at the ritzy getaway. When he was a kid growing up in the area, he used to play golf in his bare feet. And sometime in the 1990s, the *Washington Post* published a story about a secret bunker at The Greenbrier. It was called the Emergency Relocation Center, fortified housing deep underground, a safe haven for members of Congress if the Russians decided to launch the big bomb during the Cold War.

"The New River Gorge Bridge is here somewhere, too," I said. "Bungee jumping started on that bridge." I must have sounded like a tour guide talking and wasn't convinced Leslie found any of it interesting. I kept talking anyway.

"Casey bungee jumped one time. It was at an amusement park setup. I don't know where he gets the guts," I said. From the time he was little, my son loved heights, and fast and furious roller coasters. Now, on the weekends he hikes in wild country and on steep, rugged cliffs.

"Is it a suicide bridge?" Leslie asked. A few days before we left on the trip, we were talking about infamous spans where people go to take their own lives. Not sure what got us on that morbid subject, but we had looked up some facts and figures and found dozens of them across the globe. San Francisco's Golden Gate is one of the big ones, but there are others in Seattle, San Diego, and Pasadena. There are bridges in Prague, Sydney, and Montreal. And in China, from one span—the Nanjing Yangtze River Bridge—more than 1,200 people have jumped to their deaths.

"Don't know," I said. "But I do think people have died. There's this big celebration on the bridge every year. I think they call it Bridge Day, or something."

We had spanned many bridges and traveled over a few rivers on the trip so far, and I wished we had had the time to see the New River Gorge, actually cross it. But even without that side visit, there was something symbolic about crossing over or near those bodies of water. Explorers say the best way to cross a river is slowly, step by step. If you move too quickly, the current will knock you down. But we, of course, were being carried by modern transport, and although we too were explorers, I could help see this as a different kind of journey, marked by each bridge, each creek, stream, and river we crossed. And the farther east we traveled, the more we mellowed, the more we righted ourselves. There was no current that could knock us down. The frenetic start to the trip had been incrementally discarded on the west side of each of our crossings and now, the two of us, heading east with a guitar and a song were entering a brand-new part of the world, a new wilderness where we had never been, on a pilgrimage we were committed to complete, although not yet aware of it. We were on the other side of one more bridge, one more river, the sun high and bright in the sky, shining through the car windows to warm our shoulders.

Chapter 4

Leslie had taken the wheel somewhere near Beckley, West Virginia, a sleepy mountain town just off I-64. There is a street corner there where John F. Kennedy and Hubert Humphrey nearly bumped into each other back in 1960. I remembered this fact from one of the books I had read on JFK. The two were rivals for their party's presidential nomination. They recognized each other and both got out of their vehicles and chattered for a bit. Coal and the mines were two big issues back then. For us, though, the issue was gasoline. We filled up and switched drivers.

"Mind if I close my eyes for a bit?" I asked.

I hadn't slept well the previous night in the Ohio hotel. Still, despite how drained I was, I knew I wasn't going to find much comfort or rest. I'm not a very good car passenger anymore. I get anxious in the right-side seat, nervously pressing the phantom brake when the driver takes a quick turn or gets a bit too close to the car in front. This is not to say Leslie is a bad driver, or anyone else for that matter. Holding the wheel, being in control, is just more reassuring for me. I wasn't always like this. I once sat for nearly two hours in the cramped passenger seat of a tiny 1966 MG with my girlfriend in my lap, my guitar and our duffel bags stuffed in the rear compartment, and my daredevil college buddy in the driver's seat. The MG was a fixer-upper and it creaked and rattled as we raced along the back roads to the college. My friend was a good driver, but one that did not hesitate to take a risk. He once drove the MG on a campus sidewalk. Still, on this ride I was never scared, worried, or fearful all the way from Pittsburgh to Clarion State, about 120 miles. Other than my leg falling asleep twice, the drive was uneventful. I was young. We were young.

"Nap away," Leslie smiled.

"Shake me if you need to me get the wheel," I said.

For an hour or so I tossed in my seat, at times placing my head on the passenger side window. I was in and out of sleep, mostly out, and jerked and squirmed with the bumps in the road, the lane changes, and each tap of the brakes.

"How about some music?" I asked, sitting up straight in my seat, attempting to rejuvenate my body, if not my mind, and giving up on any real rest. My phone was nearly dead so we used Leslie's and plugged in her music library.

"Babe, seriously," I said. "Every song is depressing."

"This is all stuff that was before my Iowa sabbatical," Leslie said, apologizing.

Leslie had been through some difficult times. Not only did she escape two soul-sucking marriages, she also had battled cancer. Bad cancer. Stage four. She beat it. But after all of the body-numbing treatment—scarring of her body and even losing her voice for a time—she needed change, renewal. Leslie's son and daughter lived in Iowa City, so she packed up and headed three hours west, bought a home, crewed on the Iowa River, practiced yoga, and walked miles in nature to restore her spirit.

"So the music got happier in Iowa?" I asked.

"Absolutely," she said, confirming her metamorphosis.

When Leslie and I first met inside a Corner Bakery restaurant mid-morning on an early April day, one thing we immediately recognized was our mutual love of music.

"Have you heard of Dawes?" I asked, sipping my coffee at a table near the restaurant window.

"Oh, wow! You know Dawes?" she asked. "I don't know anyone our age who knows Dawes!"

The folky band weaved McCartney-like melodies with insightful lyrics, a mix of Dylan and the singer-songwriters of the Laurel Canyon days—Neil Young, Jackson Browne, Joni Mitchell. So, maybe it wasn't that unusual for two fifty-somethings to dig Dawes, but it was unusual for two people our age to even know who they were.

I didn't know the name of the artist playing through the car speakers at the time. All I could hear were the miserable tones of a despondent singer. I reached for the phone to search Leslie's library, hoping to fill the car with something a little less gloomy.

"Funny how the music we choose is the music inside our hearts at the time we choose it," I said.

The soft, gentle, fingerpicking of an acoustic guitar arose from the car's speakers, like delicately ascending smoke from a campfire at dusk.

"This is a hauntingly beautiful song," Leslie said.

Although there have been a number of interpretations suggesting Iron and Wine's "Resurrection Fern" is about the Civil Rights Movement, I'm really not sure what those tender, poetic lyrics are supposed to mean. You would have to ask the songwriter, Samuel Beam. But when I leaned back in the passenger seat to listen, there were a few things about the song for which I was certain: it was one of Leslie's favorites, it was not a downer, and the words that referred to "the oak tree and its resurrection fern"—two intertwined living things, one thoroughly dependent on the other for its survival—not only evoked a beautiful image, they reminded me of how reliant we are on each other.

"Better?" I asked.

"Better," she said.

* * *

A few weeks before the trip to Virginia and the songwriting contest, Leslie and I had been in the stands at Red Rocks Amphitheater in Colorado to see Samuel Beam (Iron and Wine) sing a solo set. Neither of us had been to a concert in years and a time since those days of dorm room joints and smoky bongs. You leave all that behind when you get old, right? But it was Colorado and the stuff was now legal.

It was a great August night in the Rockies, starry clear after a damp yet pleasing afternoon. We had hiked a few miles in a light drizzle up a rugged trail next to a creek and into a mountain meadow. We ate a light lunch and drank a lot of water to fight off altitude sickness. And afterward, we visited a marijuana dispensary just a few miles from the trailhead.

"She's not much of a smoker," I told the clerk, a young man sporting dreadlocks, a yellow bandana around his forehead, and one of those "very cool, dude" Colorado speech patterns. He told us later he was an accomplished snowboarder. It figured.

"I was thinking the edibles," I added.

"Awesome," he said. "Take a look at these." He pulled several choices from the display case behind the counter, each wrapped like a Hershey bar or Baby Ruth. I don't remember all the names, but I believe one of the edibles was called Monkey Bar—made with cocoa, small pieces of coconut, and hash oil.

"She just needs a tiny bit," I said. "Again, it's been decades."

"A lightweight," Leslie said.

"Cool," the clerk said. "Yeah, you got to go easy on this, man. Maybe just take a piece the size of your fingernail to start. Plus, it takes longer to kick in, so there's that."

Graham had taught me this fact just a couple of months before on another trip to Colorado. It had been years since I had last smoked dope. So when my son gave me a hit off of the glass pipe he had purchased at a marijuana dispensary in Denver, I immediately choked out a smoky cough.

"Harsh," I rasped.

"Gotta get used to it again," Graham said.

"I was twenty-two years old," I said, clearing my throat.

We sat around a fire at a campsite a few miles from Leadville at an elevation of somewhere around 10,000 feet. It was an early evening in August, but still a chill moving in. It can get cold high up in the Rockies no matter what time of year. We had planned the trip months before, a camping journey to Colorado, a part of the country Graham had never been. The trip was a few weeks before I was to return to regular hours at my teaching job at the college, a perfect time to drive 1,100 miles, pitch a tent, and settle in for a few days to let my beard grow, hike, and smoke legal marijuana. Yes, Graham wanted to camp in majestic mountains, but there was no question he was keen on checking out the legal dope culture. He was a proponent of legalization and a student of weed. He could rattle off the names of strains, levels of THC, and summarize legislative arguments surrounding legalization. He was passionate, schooled, and always prepared to make his point. Graham was not a stoner, a clichéd weed wizard. Instead, he took his dope seriously and was always ready to set someone straight about marijuana, the myths and realities.

"This is not Woodstock weed," Graham said. "They have to meet standards here. No mites, no mold. It's pure stuff. It's got to pass state requirements. Like prescription drugs."

"It's still smoking, though," I said. "Like an unfiltered cigarette."

I drank from a water bottle, wiped my mouth, and again lifted the pipe to my lips.

"Make sure you take it in deep. Got to keep it in your lungs," Graham said.

I was not in the habit of getting high with my son. I wasn't in the habit of getting high, period. Graham was twenty-two and I could count on one hand the number of times the two of us had shared a couple of beers, so partaking in cannabis was somewhat surreal. For his twenty-first birthday we had downed a few Bud Lights and Fireball shots along with his mother at a Steelers' bar on the North Side of Chicago, but not much since then.

"That one wasn't so bad," I said, exhaling into the crisp air.

"The taste will mellow," Graham said, educating me. "There's very little bite to this."

We sat on folding lawn chairs as the sun began to fall. Graham shared a joint with his friend Kirkland who had come along on the trip, and I puffed the pipe. We talked about music, bears, altitude sickness, and what we might cook over the fire for dinner.

"What do you see in those clouds?" Graham asked, leaning back in his chair.

White billows moved slowly across the late-day sky.

"They just look like cotton balls," said Kirkland.

I slid deeper into my chair, stretched my legs, pointed with the pipe, and asked, "Anyone see the face eating the turtle's head?"

I was officially high on legal weed in Colorado.

Now I was back and with the knowledge I had gained from Graham, I could purchase a little weed with confidence.

"You eat just a little of an edible," I said. "You can always eat more. You can't eat less once you've taken that first bite. And, be patient."

"I don't want to get goofy," Leslie said.

"Totally. But he's right. Just take a little, wait for a half hour or so, see how you feel," the clerk said. "It should be a mellow buzz, man."

I put my arm around Leslie. "I'll take care of you," I said.

We left with a Monkey Bar.

Both of us were on our phones as we entered Red Rocks. I was catching up with my older son, Casey, who lived in Seattle, and Leslie was tying up the loose ends of a real estate transaction. Leslie's career as a real estate agent began years before and she was a go-getter, but the aggression softened after the cancer and since Iowa. We parked the rental car, a red Taurus, along one of the several roads that snaked from one the amphitheater's several gates. We wanted to stay away from the big parking lots so we could skip out more quickly when the concert ended. The doors to the stands opened later than we had hoped. There had been storms in the area earlier in the day and the amphitheater had lost power, getting electricity back only an hour before the scheduled start time. Long lines had formed and the crowds moved slowly through the entrances. Once in our seats, we settled in, eager for the music.

"Take a bite?" I whispered.

"I guess it's time," Leslie said.

I broke off a chunk of the Monkey Bar, about the size of my thumb's fingernail and handed it to Leslie.

"That's not bad. Chocolaty," she said.

We had decided I was not indulging. One of us had to drive.

Houndmouth, the opening band, a country-flavored foursome was two or three songs into the set when I asked Leslie how she felt.

"Nothing," she said, as if disappointed.

Fifteen minutes passed. Still nothing.

"Here," I said. "Take another bite." I handed Leslie a second piece, a smidge smaller than the first.

Another fifteen minutes. Houndmouth was now thanking the audience and walking off stage.

"Is it supposed to take this long?" Leslie asked.

"Give it time," I said.

The intermission was shorter than usual for a rock concert. The crews were rushing to make up for the late start. Only ten minutes had passed and Samuel Beam was stepping toward the microphone with his guitar strapped around his neck.

Leslie nuzzled her cheek into my shoulder. "This is going to be awesome," she whispered.

"How you feel?" I asked.

Leslie giggled. "I think something's happening."

Three songs later, I turned toward her. Leslie was now leaning back, her body seemingly melting into her seat, her back against the bleacher behind us. "Oh, this good," she sighed. "It's nice."

Another song. Then another. And then everything changed. Leslie suddenly sat up out of her dope-induced mellowness, erect and stiff, and launched her fingernails into my thigh.

"Don't leave me."

I grabbed her hand from my leg, but she quickly snapped the other across her lap and snatched my forearm.

"You can't go. Don't leave me."

I had not moved, showed no sign of stepping away to go to the bathroom, to get a beer, or even to stand and clap.

"Babe? You okay?"

I had heard of weed-triggered paranoia, but I had never seen it up close and personal.

"Is it supposed to feel like this?" she asked, her voice now shaking, cracking.

I placed an arm on Leslie's shoulder as Beam's guitar and melancholy voice spread over the amphitheater.

"You should eat something. Let me get you something." I started to stand.

"No! Don't move." Her fingernails were again digging holes in my thigh. I placed my forehead on hers, hoping to comfort her.

"I can't be alone," she said, her hands clutching my leg and arm, as if I were a post at the edge of a cliff, the only stable, grounded thing protecting her from tumbling over the brink. *Maybe time would soothe the fear*, I thought. I put an arm around her shoulder. Her body seemed to shiver and twitch.

There are a few things to keep in mind. Leslie has no fat on her. She is lean. She is a wheatgrass eater. She doesn't digest greasy foods without feeling out of sorts. After the hike and before the concert we shared a vegetable wrap made with hummus. Not the best food to have before doing dope. My son had advised me that if you are going to get high, consume something fatty first. It had something to do with the chemistry; how marijuana's active ingredients react with your body. And although Leslie's swift shift from happy stoner to a hippie in hell was somewhat distressing, it was also a little funny. You know how it is when you are the only sober one and everyone else is wasted. It was like that.

"Can we go?" Leslie begged. "I got to go." The urgent request came just as The Head and the Heart—the concert's headliner—took the stage.

I eased Leslie down the amphitheater's long, steep steps, holding her waist the entire way. She was reluctant to use the bathroom, but somehow found the courage to let go of me long enough to scurry into the ladies room, like a nervous cat. She disappeared behind the open door and my gut twisted. *She may need someone in there,* I thought. *Panic could set in; paranoia could overtake her.* I never took my eyes off the bathroom door. Minutes past. Concertgoers with beers in their hands bustled around me, some zipping in and out of the bathrooms, others standing with friends, singing the lyrics from the song that blasted from the stage just to our right. I wanted everyone to go away, to be silent and still. Then, there she was, a sudden appearance at the exit, her eyes darting, like a wild animal in peril. I grasped Leslie's hand and we scooted down another set of steps, more quickly than I had expected her to move, and out the nearest exit as the concert's music played into the night.

Then it hit me. I had no idea where we had left the car.

We had been distracted by our phone calls when we pulled in and parked, and the only other time I had been to Red Rocks was years ago during the daylight hours. It was now nearly 10:00 pm, a big place, seemingly vast at nighttime, and my stoned and paranoid girlfriend was no help.

We walked up one road and down another, over and over, across a parking lot and up another road, again and again. Fifty yards from the amphitheater's stage, there was not a single light, no signs, no landmarks, nothing to tell where we stood in relation to anything else.

"Are we going the right way?" Leslie was now full-out trembling.

"It's okay," I said, tugging her up yet another road. "We're good. We're good."

"We're lost, aren't we? Oh, God."

The Head and the Heart's most popular song, "Lost in My Mind," could now be heard over the hillside, echoing off the mountains. And Leslie was right. I had no clue where the car was.

Fans soon began streaming from the doorways. Car engines turned over. Headlights pierced the darkness. And a long line of cabs made their way up the winding roads. I hailed one.

"We lost our car," I told the driver. Leslie and I climbed into the rear seat. "Can you help us? Drive around to look?"

"I-I-I . . . ca-ca-can't," he said, struggling to get the words out of his mouth. "Secur-cur-cur...ity won't let me g-go, go up and d-down . . . the-the-the . . . hill, the hill. Ju-just . . . one, one . . . way." Our cabbie was a stutterer.

"Damn." I said, trying to understand the rules of the roads around Red Rocks. "I guess I get that."

"Oh, God. Oh, God," Leslie moaned. In our four months of dating, I had not seen any evidence of the Leslie I was now experiencing. "This is so bad, so bad. Oh, God. Oh, God!"

"We'll find it, babe." I tried to stay confident, calm. Inside, however, all that had once been a little amusing or at first appeared as a minor setback was now beginning to carry an entirely different weight.

"Oh, God," Leslie muttered.

I handed the cabbie $10 and thanked him. He let us out in a snarl of traffic.

"We have to find someone who can help. Oh, God," Leslie insisted.

Just twenty yards down the road, a man in a reflective vest stood at one of the many intersections inside the park, ushering out slow moving cars. Maybe he could help?

"Stand over here," I said, pulling Leslie by her arm into the gravel and tall grass on the side of the road next to the hillside. She was waving her arms, nervously wiping her face, and pacing along the edge of the road, stepping dangerously close to traffic.

"No! You're going to throw me over the mountain."

For some crazy reason, Leslie was now certain I was planning to toss her over the bluff. *Damn weed.*

"You're standing in the road, babe. Jesus." I grasped her hand and dragged her close. "I'm not going to throw you over the freakin' edge, okay?" Frustration was building, but I wasn't angry. I knew I had to remain composed no matter what. At least I had to fake it. And I knew inside, this was not normal Leslie, this was weed-wacky, suspicious, distrustful, paranoid Leslie.

"That guy. That guy right there," she insisted, pointing repeatedly. "He has to know something."

"That's my plan," I said. "I'm going to talk to him."

Leslie was certain and I was hopeful that the member of the security crew now directing traffic could save us. "He can drive us around or something. Oh, God," she said.

I reached inside the pocket of my jeans for the rental car keys, thinking the company tag attached to them might have some information, maybe a license plate number, some evidence I could offer this possible savior. Before I could even approach him, Leslie spoke up.

"Can you help us, please?" she pleaded. "We can't find our car. Oh, God."

The keys were not in my right front pocket.

"What kind of car?" the guard asked, continuing to wave cars down the hill.

I reached inside the left front pocket. Nothing.

"It's red. It's a rental," Leslie said. "Oh, God."

It was as if I were riding a roller coaster about to tumble over the precipice.

"Need more than that," the guard said.

I reached for my right rear pocket, then left. Zilch. I slapped again at the two front ones, and the back ones one more time. *Son of a bitch. Did I drop the fucking keys?* I anxiously searched around my feet. There was only diffused light from the passing cars, not nearly enough to see much of anything. I knelt on the ground and wildly sifted my fingers through the roadside gravel. *Fuck.*

"The car's parked on one of the roads," Leslie explained, pacing again, circling the guard as she talked.

"Babe," I groaned.

"Let me get some more of these cars out of here first," the guard said. "We'll find it."

"Babe," I said louder.

Leslie had now planted herself directly beside the guard in the middle of the intersection, as if standing right next to this guy would be of central importance to helping our cause, as if proximity would make a difference.

"Leslie!"

Her eyes darted and she rushed toward me.

"You have the keys?"

"Oh, God. Oh, God."

"Goddamn it," I muttered. "I am so sorry."

"Oh, God. Oh, God!"

I was now certain I had left them in the cab. When I reached for my wallet to pay the driver, I must have set the keys on the seat and in my haste, never picked them up. *Fuck.*

The guard waved the final cars out of the park. He was remarkably relaxed when we told him how stupid we were. *I* was. We were apparently not the first couple to walk out of a Red Rocks' concert high and lost.

"I can find your car and I can get anything inside out for you by jimmying it open," he said, "but the cab thing, the keys, well, I don't know. What was the taxi company?"

Leslie's eyes were now glued on me for an answer.

"I think the cab was green," I said. Honestly, I had no idea.

"Oh, God."

"Wait. Wait," I added excitedly, as if I had solved a puzzle. "The driver. He stuttered. He stuttered!"

The guard hailed one of the few remaining cabs inside Red Rocks and the driver rolled down his window.

"You know a cabbie that stutters?" the guard asked.

The driver appeared as if the question was the most normal one in the world, predictable as asking for directions. "I think Johnny stutters," he said. Another taxi pulled up beside his. "Hey, Bob," the first driver called to another, "doesn't old Johnny stutter?"

"Johnny? Nah," the other driver answered, "He just kind of talks funny."

The security guard insisted we remain exactly where we were standing. "Don't go anywhere," he said. He got in his big tow truck and drove down the hill and returned minutes with the Taurus snagged onto the truck's towline, the rental's front wheels in the air. It had been only two hundred yards from where we had asked for help. The guard handed Leslie her jacket, my laptop, and a small backpack that we'd left inside the vehicle. He parked the car in the upper lot, insisting it would be safe there overnight until we figured out how we were going to handle all this. The cab ride back to Denver was $100. On the way there, Leslie threw up in my baseball cap. She was no longer paranoid; she was weed sick.

The next morning I phoned a towing company and had the Taurus moved from Red Rocks to the car rental office near the airport. Another $100. I then hired a taxi to take us to the terminal for our return flight to Chicago. That was $50.

A few weeks prior to the Colorado trip, sitting close together one evening on her living room couch, I had told Leslie I was falling in love. I was confident of my emerging feelings, but I wasn't so sure how she might see it. What comes next might seem terribly cliché, even a bit sappy, but it is exactly how it happened. Weeks after my confession, while we walked alone in the Colorado wilderness a few hours before the Red Rocks concert, moments after reaching a beautiful clearing of wildflowers surrounded by tall pines, the two of us stood alone on a narrow hiking trail in a soft mist, and Leslie told me she too was falling in love.

"You know this was just a test, don't you?" I said to Leslie, as the cab carried us along the highway to Stapleton International. "That was a mess of a night, a night no one is going to believe. The gods simply wanted to see if we could handle it."

Leslie rested her head on my shoulder, and without saying a word, she too was convinced we had aced the exam.

* * *

Somewhere along West Virginia's I-64, with the last chords of "Resurrection Fern" playing from the car's speakers, I remembered the plastic bag of leftover Colorado weed I had tucked away inside my guitar case. We were going to our own concert now, so why not pack a little dope? Plus, Leslie had said she'd give it another try as long as we stayed away from the edibles. I rested my head back against the passenger window and wondered if by chance Leslie's music library included Dylan's "Rainy Day Women #12 and 35"—you know, the song with the lyric *"Everybody must get stoned?"*

Of course it didn't. What was I thinking?

Chapter 5

What is a Best Western *Plus*? Plus *what*? The free breakfast includes grapefruit? The bedsheets are one thread silkier? Not sure I really know. But when you book a night in a Best Western, you just don't feel as confident as when you book one in a Best Western *Plus*. So, that's what I booked. It was in Waynesboro, the only available hotel room within thirty miles of Charlottesville. It was a big football weekend at the university. We thought we might explore the college town, but then we saw the brochure for all the wineries.

Central Virginia is home to hundreds of vineyards. When did that happen? Apparently when Thomas Jefferson moved to town. Here is how the story goes: Jefferson brought back some wine from France after one of his trips abroad. Then he decided to bring grapes and plant them near his new home in Monticello. It worked. The idea took off and hundreds of years later, wineries with genetic connections to the man who wrote the Declaration of Independence, thrive on the hills and in the valleys of middle Virginia.

We had quickly settled in our room and Leslie was working her way through the wine map. "I think we can hit maybe three or four of these and still get to Lovingston on time," Leslie said.

"Drunk on wine for the show," I joked. "I'm okay with that."

"But you have to play," Leslie insisted.

I sat on the small loveseat in the motel room, the guitar on my lap. I had put off the restringing long enough. I unwound the low E string from its paper packaging and stretched it along the fretboard, tugging the string's hard metal end into the bridge and pushing in the pin. The tuner drew the string taut. I skipped the A string, knowing it would be troublesome. The D, G, B, and high E went on perfectly, but as I pulled the A string across the body and slid it through the tuning peg hole, the entire tuner mechanism on the back of guitar's head fell into my lap. All of it. Every piece. The A tuner had been stripped years ago, but I'd figured a way around it. For decades, I used the lever on my metal capo like a screwdriver, placing it in the groove of the A peg, rotating it past the flaw. But now the tuner itself, the metal casing and the tiny screws that held it together had collapsed. *Really? This happens right now?* I had the other guitar, yes, but the Yamaha was my baby. It was the guitar on which I'd practiced and it sounded better than the Ovation—cleaner, crisper.

"If we start at King Family and then move south to Pollak, we'd be making our way in the direction of Rapunzel's," Leslie said, studying the notes she had taken.

I sat silently with parts of my guitar in the palm of my hand.

"That seems like a good plan, doesn't it? We could get lunch before we go," Leslie added, continuing to work through the list of wineries, checking them off with a pen.

I pulled in a deep breath and stared at the pieces of my broken tuner. For the first time, I was nervous. *All this way with one stupid song, for one stupid show, in a stupid backwoods venue, and now I was faced with a disintegrating guitar.* I started to sweat.

"Babe?" Leslie asked, turning toward me from the small desk, expecting confirmation on the plan.

"Yeah, sounds good," I said.

"Oh no," she said, noticing the pieces in my hand.

When someone shows concern over your personal predicament, you do one of two things. You either accept the concern and wallow together in the mess of it all, or you, the one with the problem, rise above it, instinctively attempting to make it all better because deep inside you don't want the other to feel as bad as you.

"Yeah, a little problem," I said. "I think I have a tiny screwdriver on my key chain."

It was delicate work. The screws were *annoying* teeny, as if made by tiny metal shop fairies.

"Do you have your reading glasses handy?" I asked.

For the next fifteen minutes, with her girly glasses on my nose, I tediously worked the pieces back into place, tightened the screws on the casing and adjusted the tuner snuggly to the guitar's head. I pulled and tugged at the tuner, testing to see if it was going to fall apart again, and slid the A string through the tuning peg. Then, using that old trick with the capo, I twisted the tuner and stretched the string, then tuned the guitar and strummed through a number of chord progressions. Strings always fall out of tune until they've settled into place. I retuned and retuned again, then strummed some more.

"You got it. Is it going to be okay?" Leslie asked.

"Yeah, it's good." I sounded more certain than I really was. "I have the other guitar, just in case. It's cool." I was doing a pretty good job of faking my worry. The tuner could decide to come apart again at any time; it's an old guitar. And there was that other concern. "I guess I should try to sing through the song again, huh?"

It had been weeks of sporadic practicing and I had yet to make it through the song without having to peek at the lyrics. Leslie was quiet about this, although I was certain she was a little anxious. I didn't want to read from a sheet. That would have been amateurish. So, as a fail-safe, I had typed out the words in small font on a couple of pieces of paper. And now, with the Scotch tape I had tossed in my suitcase before leaving, I stuck the little pieces of paper to the upper body of my guitar. If I needed it, I could glance down and grab a word or two. In all the years I had played in a band and at bars and coffeehouses decades ago, I had never done this before.

"I'm going to try playing all the way through. No help," I said.

For the first time in many days, I sang "A Better Day" without searching for words, without stopping to think, without peeking at the papers taped to my guitar. That early afternoon, some six hours before showtime, inside the Waynesboro Best Western Plus on an old guitar with a shaky A-string key, I completely nailed it. Now it was time to drink.

You have to walk through or around the grapevines to get to the door of the stately King Family Vineyards' tasting building. The big white house perfectly fits the southern charm of central Virginia, undeniably gentile. We had picked up some Panera salads before leaving Waynesboro and took them out into the open field on the edge of the winery's polo grounds with a glass of cabernet franc, a wine I had never heard of or tasted before. We were told it is made from the darkest of grapes, and apparently very French, its origins somewhere in the Bordeaux region and the legacy of the Thomas Jefferson days. And to add to the reasonable artificial sophistication, every Sunday through the summer and early fall, teams played the ancient game outside the gates to the vineyards. Polo seems so wholly English, a game of royalty, the sport of kings, but apparently its origins are in Persia, fifth or sixth century BC. The English have been known to steal everything at some point or another, and certainly a sport that involves horses was a given.

The hills in the distance were broad with color. Not a cloud blemished the sky, the grass was cool, and the wine was mellow. You could not have created a better setting. How did we get this lucky?

Then a soccer ball nearly hit Leslie in the head.

"Who brings freakin' kids to a winery?" I muttered.

It's not that this thirty something dad and his young toddler son were ruining the day, and it's not like I was being some kind of cranky, pain-in-the-ass, get-off-my-lawn old guy, it's just that I really didn't want a soccer ball zipping by, inches away, while we sipped our wine on a beautiful day, and I absolutely didn't want it to happen . . . three times!

"Seriously?" Leslie was openly agitated and wanted the soccer dad to hear her, loud and clear. Not sure he did or if he cared. Still, without being boorish, Leslie was determined this guy was going to know what she thought of his afternoon athletics.

When I was growing up, there was this old man in my neighborhood, Mr. Janiak. If you rode your bike too close to his driveway, he'd yell, "Get off my property, kid!" If his dog barked at his window as you walked by on the sidewalk, he would blame you for disturbing his mutt. And of course, don't toss a ball anywhere near his yard. Remember the guy in the movie *The Sandlot*, James Earl Jones' character? The grumpy, scary neighbor on the other side of the ball field's fence? That was Mr. Janiak; of course, without one ounce of the redeeming characteristics Jones' character would eventually reveal in the movie.

"Ah, screw it," I said, smiling and remembering old Mr. Janiak. "Just drink the wine. The soccer kid will simply disappear." We tapped our glasses in a toast and drank up.

I decided right there I didn't ever want to be *that* grouchy old guy.

As we were leaving, about a hundred yards from the parking lot, we noticed an artist with a large easel, a young woman, standing in the clearing alone. Her back faced us; her eyes on the vibrant hills. We couldn't see the canvas, but she undoubtedly was capturing the view. Leslie took a picture with her phone.

"It's beautiful, isn't it? An artist at work," she said.

A particular stillness came over us. The anticipated groove of the weekend had established itself. All the driving, the rushing, the got-to-get-there momentum of travel had now significantly decelerated. A little wine and bit of art does things.

Pollak was next, a vineyard even more beautiful than the first. White pillars upheld the roof over the flagstone patio and inside caramel-colored hardwood floors led to an elegant, crescent-shaped tasting bar. We met a couple there who had moved from Colorado to Virginia so she could take a job in the athletics department at the University of Virginia. They offered good recommendations on the wines. We drank; we laughed. There is something about wine that turns everyone into best friends.

Leslie and I had time for one more vineyard. Afton Mountain's slogan—*Grapes Don't Grow in Ugly Places*—could have been the motto for any of these vineyards. That is not an exaggeration. Maybe it seems a whitewash of the experience, but truly, each of the wineries was inviting, charming, and lovely.

"What time you have?" I had lost my perspective on the clock as we wound our way to the vineyards.

"Just before six," Leslie said, glancing at her phone. "We can stop at Basic Necessities and then be on our way. That okay?"

The photos on the Internet of the little shop showed a delightful, cottagelike restaurant, only eight tables or so, very small. The reviews said it was part of the "slow food" movement, using local farm goods. No pesticides. Free-range meats. Three women ran it. They had been friends for years. Stepping in Basic Necessities was like walking into a secret hideaway somewhere in the French countryside. Mismatched tables tucked into a small seating area, local art was on the walls, flowers from the restaurant's garden on the tables.

"Oh, I wish we had more time," Leslie said. We had thought about trying to eat here, but tables fill up on a Saturday evening and we hadn't planned our time so well. Instead, we browsed the tightly stocked shelves full of cheeses, wines, and specialty dark chocolates and burned off what was left of a minor wine buzz.

"Time?" I asked Leslie.

"We should go," she answered.

On the way out past the garden and the stone walkway, a man stepped aside to allow us through.

"Great place, isn't it?" he asked.

We told him we had not had dinner but heard it was a wonderful spot.

"Superb," he said. "Got to come back."

We explained we were only in Virginia for a couple days and had a musical appointment to keep.

"All the way from Chicago," I said, informing him and

reminding myself of the long ride.

"And you're playing tonight?" he asked.

He had heard of Rapunzel's, but he didn't appear to be the kind of guy that hung out at a music venue on a Saturday night or knew much about the music scene of central Virginia. He told us he had retired and now lived in the area after years of working in Washington, DC. He was a regular at the wineries, but not Rapunzel's.

"So what's the best way to Lovingston?" I asked, beginning to feel a bit restless about the clock.

"A left, a right, keep going. Easy to find," he said confidently. He smiled, wished us luck, and reminded us one more time. "Left, right, stay on that road."

Simple enough, I thought, and we did just as he told us. But after a few miles the road narrowed, it tumbled and turned, winding through a thickening forest, and it wasn't long before something just didn't seem right.

"Is this correct?" I asked. The sun was setting and the road had morphed into a lane. No houses, no wineries, no businesses, no road signs.

Leslie tried to pull the directions up on her phone. No signal.

"I don't remember ever being on a road like this," Leslie said, fidgeting in the passenger seat, staring at her phone, trying to will the slightest cell coverage.

"We're coming in from the other direction, right? What time is it?" I asked.

"Back the other way we passed a little store. Let's ask them," Leslie suggested.

"That means back tracking, losing more time. Don't you think?"

"It's almost 6:30. You have to be there at 7, right?"

"You pull straws or something, get a number, that's your place in the show."

I didn't want to say out loud what missing the pre-show

number selection might mean. The rules were pretty clear. Disqualification if not there on time, and here we were in the Virginia wilderness, with no phone signal, no idea where we were or even what road we were on.

It was Red Rocks all over again, minus the weed.

Chapter 6

I almost missed the birth of my first child.

My wife had been at her office and was on her way to the hospital, but first was going to make a stop at the post office to pick up a package. It was a Polaroid camera from her father, a way to capture the first photos of our first child. Marie was not going to leave it behind even with labor pains. That was Marie. A planner. A doer. She got stuff done.

Marie knew it was time. Her water had broken and if I remember correctly, contractions had started. I was at work—a radio station in Chicago—when she called to alert me. She sounded calm and together on the phone. I headed home, anxious but not panicked. I checked the mail, took the dog to the neighbors, and turned on the porch light. For some reason, whatever it was, I did not believe things were pressing; I did not feel the need to rush. I believe you are *supposed* to sense urgency. I didn't. Plus, she too had run errands on the way to the hospital—one of them was a stop at the post office to mail a package. I believe it was something for her father who lived in Pennsylvania. Maybe she believed staying busy would keep her calm. Maybe I did, too.

"There he is!" the nurse said, escorting me to the birthing room at the hospital. What I remember was her tone, the tenor of her voice, signaling my wife's state of mind, as if the nurse were channeling the uneasiness in the room.

I hate being late. For job interviews, dentist appointments, tee times. I was never late for a gig. I was an on-time kind of guy— at least I tried to be. But on that day, the birthday of my first child, I was apparently later than I comfortably should have been. I didn't have any idea when I was *supposed* to be at the hospital, truly. How do you measure these things? I'd never done this before, been an expectant father. I didn't miss the birth, thank goodness. But I cut it close, and I felt the near miss as soon as I walked into the hospital room. And now on an unknown narrow road in the fading light of a fall evening in the Virginia hills, the awful feeling of cutting it close for my son's entrance into the world was on my mind because I believed I might be about to miss another important moment. Not one equivalent to my son's birth, of course. Nowhere close. But still, the anxiety of the moment was just as palpable.

"Excuse me," I said, attempting to interrupt a conversation between the clerk, an older Asian man standing behind the cluttered counter of the convenience store, and a young couple, a man and a woman who appeared to be aimlessly searching for the wine aisle. I heard one of them say something about pinot noir.

All three quickly turned in my direction as if I had just screamed, "Boo!"

"Know how to get to Lovingston?" I asked urgently.

What happened next was like something from a Marx Brothers movie, a Three Stooges short. Simultaneously the clerk pointed in one direction and the couple, as a unit, pointed in the exact opposite.

"No, no, no," said the man from the couple, directing his correction at the clerk. "We just came from there."

The clerk shook his head. "Wrong," he said, employing an index finger from each hand to point the other way.

"We were just in Lovingston," the man from the couple continued.

It was then that I noticed the accent. English? Irish?

"We're visiting. Mapped it out," the woman said.

"I live here," the clerk said, scolding the woman.

That was enough for me.

"Hey, thanks," I said, backing up through the door and outside.

Jesus! Un-fucking believable.

"What'd they say?" Leslie asked, as I hurriedly stepped back into the driver's seat.

"No one knows a damn thing," I muttered.

I turned the car toward the edge of the convenience store parking lot and nervously contemplated.

Leslie fumbled with her phone again. Still no cell coverage. "Wait, wait. There's that wine map!"

Looking one way down the road and then up the other, I pulled out, the car almost screeching in the direction of Basic Necessities, the opposite of where we had been a few minutes before.

"Where you going?" Leslie asked.

"We got to choose," I said. "Let's just make a decision and get on with it."

Leslie pulled the wine map from her purse, unfolded it, and quickly decoded the red, blue, and black roadways. "We're good. We're good! Keep going," she said, pointing at the map. "I see it. This is right."

I didn't dare ask the time.

* * *

I've had a long career in broadcasting, an agonizingly time sensitive business. Seconds. Minutes. Time, time, time. Before I was married, I was visiting my soon-to-be wife over a weekend. She lived and worked in Cleveland at the time. I was in Pittsburgh working as a morning radio news anchor. I decided to stay over Sunday night and leave early enough Monday morning to arrive at the station by 5:00 am. But things didn't work out that way. Again, I remember the details because I so dislike being late. I either didn't set the alarm or ignored it and woke up in Cleveland at 4:00 am. It's a two-and-a-half hour drive. I traveled at 80 mph most of the way but still missed the first newscast at 6:00 am by five minutes. In the broadcast business, one is not supposed to be late. Ever. So with this event in my past, there should be no surprise that for decades I have had a recurring dream about being late for a radio show. It's not quite like what actually happened, but it's close. I walk into an empty studio, a turntable needle rhythmically skips at the center end of a vinyl record, the last part of the analog tape of an old-fashioned reel-to-reel slaps against the tape heads. There is a dreadful silence from the monitors. I push the button for the microphone and it will not turn on. Nothing. I'm not only late, there is not only dead air, but I am helpless to do anything about it.

In the big scheme of things, being late for a songwriting competition is not crucial to one's overall life. Being late for the last helicopter out of Saigon in 1975 or the final spaceship back to our galaxy, *that's* crucial. There is nothing life threatening or dangerous in being a few minutes late for a gig, even though this gig meant a lot to me. However, there was a time many years ago when I thought I wanted to live a riskier life, one in which the element of time or timing could be critical. For a few years early in my broadcast career while working as a news director at a Pittsburgh radio station, I considered what it would be like to be a foreign correspondent, a war reporter. Not that I had any offers. Still, I was captivated. I read Graham Greene's *The Quiet American* and accounts of Hemingway's time in Spain. I listened to old broadcasts of Edward R. Murrow on the rooftops in London. It seemed so glamorous and daring. It wasn't, of course. War and the foreign correspondents I met later in my life would set me straight on that, but they admitted adrenaline and idealism had fueled them. And they reminded me that timing was everything, being at the right place at the right moment, choosing the right conflict at the right time in history, and making those choices at the right period in your life. It's a young person's job. Old men don't cover wars. When you are young, you believe you are immortal, invincible. Deep down you are convinced you will live forever. Case in point: a friend, a broadcast colleague once asked me to go with him to Spain to run with the bulls, something I had romanticized about. I was a Hemingway fan. It was my fortieth year on the Earth—in between young and old—and as a birthday gift my then-wife, who certainly knew my passions, had considered sending me to Pamplona or a long week in Scotland to play golf with my father. It was my choice. My buddy got on a plane to Spain. I got on a plane to Glasgow. I cherished my time in Scotland with my father; I would never give it back. But, I admit, I still long for the bulls.

"There it is!" Leslie said, pointing through the windshield.

Late no longer mattered. My phone read 6:56.

Rapunzel's was a big red barn of a building with gigantic white letters painted on the side: LIVE MUSIC, ESPRESSO, BOOKS. Although we couldn't see the words in the evening darkness, we knew they were there from the photos we had seen of the place. Tightly parked cars lined both sides of the street, a swarm of musicians carrying guitar cases stood near the side entrance.

"No turning back now, as they say." I slid my guitar case off the rear seat and shut the car door.

"This is so cool," Leslie said, looking back toward Rapunzel's, floodlights illuminating the building's edges. "You have every-thing?" she asked.

I nodded. *Yes. Yes, I did.* I walked toward the door, my guitar case swinging in my hand. A wave of relief passed over me and along with it a tremendous sense of deliverance. I was twenty-five again with the world in front of me, all its possibilities, all its promise, as if Rapunzel's was my personal fountain of youth.

"You must be Bob?" I asked, reaching out to shake the hand of a man wearing a black fedora. Bob was a white-haired, white-bearded, red-faced man, wearing jeans and a well-worn unstruc-tured sport coat, standing just inside the dimly lit entranceway. Bob was the one who first informed me that I had been chosen a finalist. It came in a simply worded email:

Dear David

It is our pleasure to inform you that your song has been selected as a finalist entry in Rapunzel's 12th Annual Songwriting Contest.

"That's me," Bob said, grinning. "And you are?"

"Dave Berner. 'To a Better Day,'" I felt required to announce the song's title.

"Oh, yes. You're from Chicago." Bob scanned his clipboard and checked off my name. "We're going to gather all the finalists in a few minutes. Pleasure to have you," he said.

Leslie clutched my arm, as if to punctuate our current reality. We had overcome the lousy time management and beaten worthless directions; we had fought off angst and tension. We were at Rapunzel's and with me was the only woman in the world I would have wanted next to me for this night. Leslie was my advocate, far from a mere cheerleader.

We found a table near the front just off stage left.

Rapunzel's was bigger than I had expected. The stage was high and deep. There were lights and a sound mixing board and big speakers. Tables and chairs of all kinds were scattered around, some in tucked-away spots next to walls lined with shelves of used books and covered in paintings and artwork. Battered and dinged hardwood made up the floors. Even the venue's dog—a bushy mutt with deep brown eyes—was a lovely, matted mess. Rapunzel's was delightfully untidy, as if all of the thousands of songs played there over the decades had hung in the air and fallen into the crevices of worn, overstuffed chairs, and all those dusty books; music that would forever live in the corners and cracks.

I leaned my guitar case on the wall beside the stage and rested the Yamaha against the case, the same guitar I had played at an intimate coffeehouse performance at Duquesne University back in 1975. The same one I played at a wedding reception in the old Waldorf Astoria Hotel in Pittsburgh in 1978. The same guitar that rested on my knee when I sat on a stool and sang Willie Nelson's "Crazy" inside a smoky Pittsburgh bar on a Friday night in the summer of 1980, my angel-voiced then-girlfriend singing harmony. There were scuffs and bruises on its body, finger-worn frets, and that nagging, damaged tuner. But even with all of this wear and the dozens of replacements I had considered over the years, the guitar was still right beside me, still resonating the decades of notes it had produced. The guitar had earned its place that night at Rapunzel's.

"They gave us these ballots," Leslie said, handing me one. The printed page had each performer's name, song name, and a place for comments. There were three final judges for the competition—one from a local radio station—but everyone at the event had their say in the popular vote, which also had weight toward choosing a winner. "Check out this name," she said.

One composition was titled "The X in Sexy."

"That should be interesting," I said.

"And isn't this guy here the one that won second place last year?" Leslie asked, pointing to a name on the sheet. Gene Mills seemed the real deal; a bearded, middle-age man with a sweet voice and a knack for good melodies. I had found a YouTube video of him playing his entry from the previous year. He was a good performer, and he was also what mattered most on this night—a good songwriter.

"Tough competition," I said.

"Well, they haven't heard yours yet," she said.

Before too long, all the musicians were called up a narrow, creaky set of stairs to a smaller performance space on the second floor. We stood against the walls as Bob called out our names, taking attendance. There were twenty-eight listed finalists, one had cancelled at the last moment and another had not yet arrived, but Bob dismissed the tardiness. "He'll be here," he said. "He said he's coming." The songwriter must have been a local, and I guessed locals got a pass on being late. I was still convinced I would not have.

In the near corner of the room stood a James Dean look-a-like—a tall, skinny kid with slicked back dark brown hair, his jeans rolled at the ankles. He did not have a hard pack of Marlboro Reds tucked in his shirt sleeve, but he should have. There was a Neil Young impersonator, probably in his early twenties. This was the Neil of the *Harvest* album—long, stringy hair, torn jeans, T-shirt, and open flannel shirt. An Appalachian mama with a yardstick-straight mane and a flowing sundress held a lap harp in her hands. Beside her was a pudgy man wearing a blue button-down shirt, neatly ironed khakis, and accountant's eyeglasses. He looked like your dad's insurance agent friend and he swayed nervously. Next to me stood a young woman, probably in her mid-twenties with purple streaks in her hair, and piercings in her nose and ears. She wore a tank top over big breasts and a portly torso, her bare arms sporting intricate tattoos. One of them was a dragon, I think. Another woman, a few years older, leaned against the far wall in her own imaginary row just behind the others. She looked like the twenty-something woman you might see at the Wal-Mart checkout register. There were hippies, punks, and freaks; cowboy hats, baseball caps, and bandanas; Doc Martins, Nikes, boots, and loafers; beards, receding hairlines, and lengthy locks on gals and guys.

And then there was me—faded blue jeans, a black V-neck sweater with a checkered sky blue shirt underneath. I wore dark brown Timberland boots. On my left wrist was a leather braid bracelet; attached to it was a round piece of bone, the ancient black spiral symbol etched in the center. My shoulder-length brown hair had disappeared years ago, leaving behind a bald head with closely cropped gray on the sides and sideburns to my ear lobes. The full beard of my twenties was now a salt-and-pepper goatee. To most of the musicians in the room, I'm certain I looked more like a high school English teacher than a folk singer. Maybe that was a mistake. Maybe I should have worked harder at playing the role—pierced an ear, allowed for a week's worth of beard stubble, or let the little hair I had grow out to sport a bald man ponytail.

Small pieces of paper had been tossed in a black hat. Written on each was a number, from one to twenty-eight. Our blind picks would determine the order of the performances. I chose twelve, right in the middle of the pack.

Chapter 7

Judge Dread was an Englishman and an unlikely reggae singer, the first white recording artist to have a hit in Jamaica. When people came to his concerts to hear his music without ever seeing him before, they were stunned to find a chunky white guy on stage. Most of his music was banned from the BBC because of the sexual innuendos; it was kind of his shtick. Despite that, Dread was able to catch the ear of Elvis Presley. The King had planned to record a song Dread wrote, a clean one called "A Child's Prayer" as a Christmas present for his daughter, Lisa Marie. Elvis died in 1977 before getting into the studio to lay it down. Twenty-one years later, Dread died. And here's the epic part: he died on stage. The singer-songwriter had a heart attack while waving to his fans after a performance in 1998 at the Penny Theatre in Canterbury.

If you're going to be a singer-songwriter—a rock 'n' roller—isn't dying on stage the grandest exit ever?

Rock star deaths are time stamps for so many of us. Who could argue the impact and defining significance of John Lennon's death? Jimi Hendrix, Janis Joplin, Jim Morrison, Kurt Cobain, Buddy Holly, Keith Moon, John Bonham, three Lynyrd Skynyrd band members? Guns, drugs, plane crashes, suicides—the more violent or unexpected, the more captivating. It's morose, odd, kind of creepy, but rock fans still visit Jim Morrison's grave in Paris; they still show up to view the plane crash site near Clear Lake, Iowa, where Buddy Holly, Ritchie Valens, and the Big Bopper died; they flock to the old home of Kurt Cobain at 171 Lake Washington Boulevard in Seattle; and light candles every December 8 outside The Dakota in New York where Mark David Chapman shot John Lennon. But with all the fascination, and all these deaths, there are few stories of rock stars actually dying while performing.

For whatever reason, this was what was in my head minutes before the start of the competition at Rapunzel's. *What if I died up there singing my song?*

Certainly, I wasn't planning on such a thing. I wasn't sick or ill. I didn't have some death wish. But dying up there would certainly mean immortality, wouldn't it? Weird thought, huh? It was fleeting; I didn't dwell on it. Still, it was there.

I've only been to one place where a rock legend has died — Graceland. My son Graham and I visited Memphis years ago. We saw Sun Records, too, which I found more interesting than Elvis's home. Graham was impressed with the microphone on a stand in the corner where Elvis, Dylan, Bono and dozens of other stars sang and recorded their songs. An X marked the spot in the small studio at Sun. Graceland, on the other hand, was rundown; there was sadness about it, like the dusty old worn-out home of a distant relative. The upstairs where Elvis' body was found is off limits. Seeing that section of the house might have changed my mind about the Graceland visit. It sounds morbid, but the upstairs is what everyone wants to see.

* * *

The line at Rapunzel's bar was long. Some performers sat quietly on chairs or stood against the walls, others appeared to be catching up with old friends, and a few had pulled from the cases the instruments they would soon cradle on stage — guitars, mandolins, fiddles, harmonicas. Some played their instruments, some sang softly, and some, like me, tried to tune. But the unexpected wail of a child nearby made it a difficult to hear the notes.

"Babysitter cancelled," the young woman said, "so, here we are."

She was maybe in her early twenties, wearing a hippie sundress and if it had been the right time of year, I have no doubt she would have had flowers in her hair. Her husband—maybe her boyfriend—was the musician. His hair was pulled back in a ponytail and he carried a Martin acoustic by the neck. The child was a mop-headed kid and was clearly overstimulated. All the people, the lights, the music, the noise was a lot for a little guy to take in.

"We just couldn't miss this, though," the woman added, snatching her son by the back of his pants before he could run off.

"Kind of cool that he gets to experience it," Leslie said.

When I first got word that I had made the list of finalists, I immediately contacted Leslie. My sons learned about it next. I telephoned Casey in Seattle. He wished me luck and asked a lot of questions about what kind of competition I'd be facing. At the time, these were questions for which I had no answers. I told Graham about the contest by first playing my song over the car speakers as the two of us headed out on a Friday evening to an early dinner.

"What do you think of this song? Listen to it all before you say anything."

Graham had eclectic tastes—Credence Clearwater Revival, Bob Dylan, and even George Michael were on his 3,000-song iPhone playlist. But more than anything, he was a heavy metal fan. I didn't have much hope he'd think much of my folksy little song.

Graham stretched back into the passenger seat and tilted his head, as if to better hear the music. He remained silent until the last chord rang out.

There was a beat of quiet. "That was strong," he said.

"Really? You liked that?"

"Yeah, seriously. It's you, right?"

"Yep, it's your dad."

"Cool. You didn't suck," he joked.

"Now what would you say if I told you that song is a finalist in a competition?"

"Come on?"

"Yeah and I have to go to Virginia to play it on stage."

"Fucking no way!"

"But I'm not sure I should go."

"What? What the hell?"

"Well, it's a long way and it'll cost money."

Graham turned to look at me as I drove along the road to the restaurant. "I will fucking destroy you if you don't go. You *have* to go." Graham played drums. Music was our biggest connection. He didn't joke about music.

"Would you go with me?" I asked.

I had my concerns about Graham taking time out from his part-time job and college classes, but my heart wanted him there.

"You know," said Graham, contemplating it for a moment, "I really appreciate you asking me. But I think this is what *you* have to do. This is *your* dream." Then he paused and added, "Take Leslie."

"You know how we are with music, you and me," I said.

"Yeah, I get that. But this is *your* journey. It's all you. Go for it."

"You know," I said, thinking for an instant, "I think I will."

"I'm proud of you, man," Graham said, reaching out his hand to shake mine as I pulled the car into a parking space. "Really. This is awesome."

Seeing that young family with the toddler Inside Rapunzel's, I couldn't help to remember the evening in my car with Graham, playing the song for him and his firm, honest handshake.

* * *

For whatever reason, the start time for the show was delayed. Maybe they were waiting for that final performer to show up. I stood in the bar line and ordered a couple of beers for Leslie and me. Then we took a longer look around the place. One hallway near the restrooms was a kind of walk of fame—photos of past performers filled the wall space. A quick once-over revealed no famous faces, but that didn't matter. I no longer needed validation, no longer sought a good reason for being there or believing in what I was doing. I had done this before. I had performed in front of people, sang songs and played instruments to crowds large and small, albeit decades ago. Those past experiences, those long-held sensibilities had resurfaced and I was in a familiar place, one I had long forgotten or had gone missing in the insidious smog of aging.

"When I used to play guitar alone and with my band at bars and all that," I said, eyeing a black-and-white publicity photograph on the wall of a young guitarist who undoubtedly had musical dreams, "I thought I was pretty hot shit."

"I'm sure you guys were good," Leslie said.

"Yeah, *pretty* good," I said. "I wonder where those guys are now?"

I hadn't talked to the lead guitarist, Rich, in some fifteen years. I had seen him last at my father's funeral. Jeff, the bassist, disappeared a few years after the band broke up, so it had been decades since speaking with him. I had no clue where he ended up, or even if he was alive. I had heard the drummer, Dave, had moved to a small Pennsylvania town after college, married soon afterward, and worked his way to early retirement after a career in retail management. Sears, maybe? *What would those guys think of me on this night? Would they be cheering me on? Would they want to get the band back together?* A sense of sadness came over me. Memories are messy, like the inside of that rarely opened closet in the spare bedroom. Sometimes it's better to leave the door shut.

And then those peculiar thoughts of dying on stage returned.

Like old Judge Dread, Tiny Tim—the "Tiptoe Through the Tulips" guy—also dropped dead leaving the stage. Heart attack. It happened in Minneapolis for a benefit concert. Okay, not a big rock star, but a one-time celebrity, certainly. In 1954, blues guitarist Johnny Ace got boozed up and between sets he shot himself in the head. As the story goes, he was playing Russian roulette to impress some woman backstage. There was also this Italian actor, Renato Di Paolo, who was playing Judas in a play on the day before Easter in a theatre outside Rome. During the hanging scene, Di Paolo hanged himself. Accident? Suicide? He wasn't a rocker, but still, it was a death on stage. His fifteen minutes of fame were his last.

Death has always been a peculiar thing with me. I cannot tell you the date of my father's last breath. I was there, inside his home in the last hours. It was late evening, that I remember. But the date, the day of week, I do not recall. My mother's death was in December in a metal nursing home bed. But the exact date? Not sure. All those details are closeted, closed off. It's not that I avoid grief or the discussion of death. It doesn't scare me. Leslie had brawled with the Grim Reaper when cancer threatened her life, and I have embraced talking with her about those terribly difficult days. Her openness is heroic. So, I'm not trying to hide from death. But why was I having a fascination with it on the night of a songwriting competition in Virginia? Was it the connection between death and art?

The two are strange cousins, it seems. Death is a theme, a key plot element in so many films, in theater, certainly opera. And it is everywhere in literature, of course. Dylan Thomas's "Do Not Go Gentle into That Good Night" is a defiant poem about the powerlessness of growing old and edging toward one's final moments. But it is also about life and how we live it. Thomas demands that we move through this world with passion and joy. We should live a full life and when it's time to die we should go kicking and screaming. But Thomas does not denigrate death. He refers to it as the "good night" and insists, "wise men" know "dark is right." So why resist with such fervor? The answer is in living a life that rejects regret. Do not live a life of inaction, and if we believe we have, then we should fight the "dying of the light" because we have much more to live for. My mother's death after a long battle with dementia at the age of seventy-four was a tender one. Over several days, I watched her organs slowly fail—her heart gently lose its rhythm. Death was kind, quiet. I believe she never felt the need to fight it. My father's death, however, was a battle to the end. Over a couple of years, he first had bypass surgery, then gallbladder removal, then kidney stones, and then aggressive prostate cancer. The cancer got him. Even in his final moments, curled in a fetal position in his bed at my parents' home under hospice care, my father "raged." He had much left to do in his life; he wanted more of its joy. It was not regret that fueled his rage, it was the beautiful act of living. The poem undeniably focuses on how Thomas believes all of us should live our lives and how we should die, but it is also intensely personal and this may be why it resonates so deeply with so many, and certainly with me. In the last stanza, Thomas reflects on his complicated relationship with his father, and demands that he not die quietly, not simply fade away.

Was this what all those thoughts of death were all about? There I was at what might be labeled extreme middle age, the survivor of a heart attack and carrying a familial history of death at a relatively young age, and yet I was about to fulfill a young man's dream. In my own way that night, I was "raging against the dying of the light," embracing the passion and joy of life. Death will come—to me, to all of us—but on that Virginia night, with music to play before hundreds of people, I was going to live.

Chapter 8

There were four folding chairs in the cramped green room, three on one side and a single one on the other. I was seated across from Bob who sat in the single chair, holding in his lap the clipboard with the list of singers and songs. The glare of the stage lights made it impossible to see the crowd. From my position just off stage left, I could view only the performers' backs. A singer-songwriter named Kathleen Kraft, accompanied by a guitarist and a standup acoustic bassist, played a composition entitled "Evie." I assumed that was a woman's name, short for Evelyn. It was a pretty, country-flavored song, but the essential elements of the tune—the lyrics, the tempo, and the tenor of Kathleen's voice—were undistinguishable to me. In the swirl of her music, I was focused only on trying to keep my guitar in tune. Resting the body on my lap, I plucked the strings and angled my right ear low toward the sound hole, straining to hear each individual note.

Bob leaned toward me. "Quite a night, isn't it?" he whispered.

"It is," I whispered back, continuing to softly pluck.

"I'm always amazed at the diversity of the songs," Bob said, glancing out to the stage.

I smiled but purposely did not verbally respond. I wanted Bob to stop talking.

"Such quality stuff. Lot of good songwriters," Bob continued. "When you going back to Chicago?"

"Tomorrow."

"So you won't have time to see more of the area?"

"Did today." I lifted my guitar toward my chin and rested the side of my head on the body. I still couldn't hear the strings and I couldn't pluck them any louder for fear of interfering with Kathleen's song. Bob kept talking.

"It's those wineries," Bob persisted. "Beautiful and damn

good grapes." Bob didn't look like a wine drinker. He looked like a whiskey guy.

"Uh-huh." *Please, stop talking,* I thought. Could he not get the hint? What I certainly didn't want seconds before going on stage was idle chatter.

The crowd applauded and Kathleen waved to the audience. "Thank you," she said softly into the microphone, the sound echoing at the back of the stage.

"You're next," Bob said, standing from his chair. Kathleen and her accompanists squeezed past Bob, and around the chairs and me.

"Nice job," I said. They smiled confidently and moved to a small kitchen area behind the green room where one of Rapunzel's employees, a young blonde woman was handing out bottles of water to the singers.

Bob stepped to the middle of the stage. "Next up is David W. Berner," he said, studying his clipboard, glancing back at me, and then looking into the lights and out to the crowd. "His song is 'To a Better Day.'"

I had to audition for my high school band when I was in ninth grade. I was a trombone player and not a very good one. I sat in a room alone with the bandleader, Mr. Gump, a gruff taskmaster who wore a rumpled white shirt, black tie, and silver tie clip. I hadn't practiced much. Not sure why, probably was just lazy about it. Maybe I didn't want it enough. Still, I passed the audition, barely. Years afterward, I realized Mr. Gump had been quite generous. The audition was a test, an exercise; it really wasn't a definitive determining factor on whether I'd make the school band or not, and frankly, I think he kind of liked me for some reason. Only years after I had passed did I start to see how Mr. Gump, deep down, had been a bit of a softy. Good old Gump had cut me a break. But now at Rapunzel's, *no one* was going to cut me any sort of break. I'd played a lot of songs with my guitar in front of a lot of people, that had been established, but never before the critical sneer of discerning judges who did not know me from Adam and were listening for every tiny melodic defect; never before a crowd that was pitting my song against twenty-eight others and ranking with surgical judgment its emotional and musical impact, if it had any at all. At the judge's table at Rapunzel's, there was no Mr. Gump.

I took my seat on a single chair positioned front and center, and adjusted the microphone. I searched for Leslie in the blinding shimmer of lights.

"This good?" I asked, speaking into the microphone and strumming my guitar. I squinted through the lights and saw the soundman in the back behind all the seating give me the thumbs-up.

When we chose order numbers earlier that night, I was asked whether I wanted to stand or sit on stage. Instinctively, I said, "sit" because this is how I now played the guitar, seated on the couch or a living room chair. I wondered, though. *Should I be standing? There's more energy standing. Young people stand to sing. Old people sit. Well, not always. I saw Neil Young when he was in his thirties perform an entire acoustic concert sitting in a simple wooden chair. Yeah, but, hold on. I'm not Neil Young. Jackson Browne stands when he plays guitar. Still does today and he's in his sixties. I'm not THAT old. Yet. But most young players I admire—Colin Meloy of the Decemberists for one—stands and he's cool, and a modern, masterful lyricist.*

I stayed in the chair.

"I may be the one singer tonight who traveled the longest to get here," I said to the crowd. "Anyone from farther away than Chicago?"

All I could hear was a soft murmur, and for a second I thought maybe no one could hear me. Then someone yelled "Annapolis!" *Well,* I thought, *that's not that far. Can't someone do better?*

"Twelve hours and I'm happy to be here," I said, and thought again how I probably should have decided to stand. "I wrote this song about my two boys. Hope you like it."

For the first time that night, in that moment, I was completely, utterly alone. But that was not a bad thing. It was a solitary tranquility, a private peace. All that mattered right then was my guitar, my voice, and the words I had written. Worries about remembering lyrics or whether the guitar's strings were in perfect harmony, or that faulty, falling apart tuner had vanished. The stage lights went away, the foggy faces in the crowd melted, and those fresh steel strings rang out like church bells, alerting parishioners to come and rejoice, to be part of a gathering of the spirit. It was not as if I believed my song was some inspiring sermon, a homily that would convert the masses. I had no pretense about how my little ditty might move people. It was just a song. But in that moment, "To a Better Day" was a prayer, one I was singing to *me*, for *me*, a beautifully selfish act and if all those before me wanted to share in three minutes of personal expression, they were welcome. But be certain, I was picking, strumming, and singing for *my* soul, *my* redemption.

I plucked and picked through the song's opening and bent into the microphone.

Whispers wait for the darkened night
Sunken sun has faded blue
Silence cries from a weighted heart
But it is all this day has left for you.

* * *

Several summers before this performance, I had spent two months inside a small cottage in Orlando. It had once been the home of Jack Kerouac, the place where he wrote "The Dharma Bums." I was privileged to be the writer-in-residence for a time. But while I was working on a book, I also found inspiration to write music again after many years. I penned "To a Better Day" in one night, sitting on the small couch before an unusable brick fireplace in the old wooden, tin-roof home. I was eating take-out sushi and sipping wine. My sons—Graham and Casey, both in their late teens—had been struggling with personal identity, their places in the world. Not uncommon for this age, but yet when you're in the moment, and these are your children, it weighs heavily, not to mention the mark it was leaving on each of them. And there I was more than a thousand miles away, feeling helpless, believing I was a selfish parent, and more than anything, wondering what I could possibly do, if anything, to ease the burden for them.

Alone inside in deepest dreams
Far from all that is true
Melancholy melody
And a harmony that's mellowed you.

* * *

By the time of the Virginia trip, my sons had persevered and progressed to much better places. Casey had graduated from the University of Missouri, moved to Seattle to work in video production, and was discovering his passions. Graham was back in college after some early stumbles. He had finally found his focus—teaching—and was navigating his way to that realization. They were creating their own paths, their own identities, and had found balance again.

CHORUS:
But there's a light on the western sky
The setting day has left its mark
And to your surprise, the sun will rise
To a better day.

Although the song had been written about them, and for them, now years later, the song had taken on much more meaning, or so it seemed. Singing the words that night, I found strength in the performance of it, a cleansing reflection of sorts.

Not because of what the song once represented, but what it could mean for the future, for my boys, for me, for anyone. Yes, at Rapunzel's I was singing for myself, no doubt, but the message was for anyone, really. The song was not only mine or my sons' but everyone's. That night, "To a Better Day" had gone out into the world. It was no longer only playing inside my mind, my heart, but it was airborne, falling note by note like soft rain on to the hearts of anyone who wanted to listen.

Gone is the dust of a weary soul
No one clears it but you
No more scars behind hidden doors
There's only one thing left to do.

I was not the best songwriter that night, certainly. I was nowhere close. But I was center stage, offering up my emotions, expressing an intimate interior glimpse of shared humanity. I don't want to sound like I had some holy epiphany. It wasn't quite that. But as I was singing every word, playing every note, fueled by reserves of faith in my own private revitalization, the old man in me was becoming young again—even if it was only for a brief flash in time.

Sing out loud your spirit's song
Let the moon be your guide
Find the place that sets you free
There is nowhere left to hide.

What we believe we are when we're young is only the initial sketch of the forthcoming portrait. That was true for my boys and now for me.

CHORUS:
The sun has faded from the western sky
The stars rising high above the clouds
And to your surprise, the sun will rise
To a better day.

When the last chord rang out, I searched again for Leslie. I just needed to see her eyes. She was leaning forward in her seat and smiling. I smiled back.

"Thank you for listening to my song," I said to the clapping crowd. I waved, and stood from the chair. There was a high-pitched whistle from the back of the room. Bob was now standing behind me. "Nice," he said. *He probably said that to everyone,* I thought, *but at least at that moment the tiny accolade was for me alone.*

"Appreciate it," I said. I had no idea if the performance was truly "nice" or not. I had not heard the stage monitor very well, playing purely by gut and instinct, and I was no honest judge, anyway. But I did not need the lyrics that had been taped to the guitar, and I had not had to pick up the pieces of a flawed tuner from the stage floor.

What happened next, I honestly do not remember. There is a blank spot in my memory. I know that I walked off stage left and I must have squeezed through the small green room area just as all the other songwriters had, and I'm sure I was handed a water bottle, like all the others. What I do recall is leaning my guitar against a nearby wall and stepping inside a backstage restroom, tilting my body toward the mirror and looking at my eyes. I was wearing the face of a windstorm—my cheeks flushed, my body collapsed, evidence of both the flow of adrenaline and the damage from exhaustion. I put my hands under the faucet and lifted cold water to my face, not splashing it but softly applying it instead. Then, I did it a second time and again stared into the mirror. I did not recognize the person in the reflection. I did not know him. He was either the forgotten me or the new me; a neglected friend or a stranger; a songwriter or a sorry pretender. I had no intention of analyzing my place in the world while alone in a tiny unisex bathroom backstage at a music venue in central Virginia at the age of fifty-seven after a performance I never dreamed would happen, but there I was doing just that. *Who is that guy?*

When I was around ten years old, my idols were baseball players. Roberto Clemente and Bill Mazeroski of the Pittsburgh

Pirates—of that surprising World Series team of the 1960 season—were gods to me. I wanted to be them. But in my teenage years, those heroes faded and I no longer worshipped men with bats. Instead, I revered men with six strings strapped across their bodies. Then, I became a husband and father, and my musical heroes began to play hide-and-seek, disappearing behind the fog of my manufactured responsibility and duty, stepping out only for brief, private moments. And now, peering into that bathroom mirror at Rapunzel's, I could see those musical heroes standing behind me like shadowy ghosts. Just over my shoulder, emerging from my past were the visions of Bob Dylan and Stephen Stills and Neil Young and James Taylor and Paul McCartney and dozens of others, each one of them watching over me like a super-group of guardian angels.

"You absolutely killed it," Leslie said, squeezing my hands and shaking them for emphasis. She squinted, as if holding back the emotions behind her eyes, and moved her chair closer to where I had returned to my seat. "That was truly . . . incredible."

I sighed, unable to say anything.

"Let's take a short intermission now," Bob said into the micro-phone, from the stage. "Fifteen minutes. And please give our songwriters so far tonight another round of applause."

I quickly stood, took Leslie by the hand, and guided her through rows of seats and tables, darting past the bar and out into the night.

"Where are we going?" Leslie asked. "What are you doing?"

I moved out to the sidewalk, away from the smokers puffing on the patio near the entrance, and reached in my front pocket.

In my hand, I held a small black plastic container. "A little of this sounds like a really good idea right now."

"You brought that?" Leslie asked.

I had not told Leslie about the weed I had stashed in my guitar case, weed from the weekend at Red Rocks.

"And this, too," I said. In the other hand was a yellow Bic

lighter, and the small glass pipe I had purchased in Colorado when I was there camping with my son.

Leslie and I hustled along the road several blocks from Rapunzel's entranceway lights and up a long driveway to a dark, secluded parking lot behind a large real estate office, holding hands and laughing like teenagers.

Chapter 9

I'm sure Bernerd Harris is a nice guy. Probably good to his kids, loves his wife, visits his mother on Sundays. But taste is a difficult thing to define, and Bernerd's taste was clearly not mine, and not Leslie's. Still, there he was, singing his heart out.

"You put the X in sexy!" he bellowed, hopping from one foot to the other, strumming with pride and in the style of a song Weird Al Yankovic might have acknowledged with great envy.

"Seriously?" Leslie asked.

"All kinds," I said.

There is nothing wrong with a silly little tune. It did make the finals, right? And for what it was worth, Bernerd sang it with panache. Maybe it was just Bernerd himself that threw me off balance. Bernerd looked like that science teacher in middle school, the one with the big belly and the receding hairline, and the goofy laugh; the one who spoke in puns and played Dungeons and Dragons on the weekends and made sure he told everyone that he was vying for a spot in a national D&D competition. I don't mean to be judgmental or criticize Bernerd's songwriting, but when you author and perform a song entitled "The X in Sexy," well, what do you expect?

Bernerd received a solid round of applause and good for him.

"Hey, wait a minute," Leslie said, as sexy Bernerd walked from the stage, her eyes darting around our small table, then to the floor and under the chair. "My ballot?"

During the intermission, someone, we assumed, had snatched Leslie's ballot, the one given to each one of us as we entered Rapunzel's.

"Did you see my ballot on the table here?" she asked the man sitting nearby.

He shrugged his shoulders.

"Really? Come on. I left it right here."

I stood and searched behind us and under the table again.

"Someone took my ballot," Leslie said.

"Well, that's kind of a crappy thing to happen," I said. "It's not in your pocket, your purse?"

"Nope," she said, tapping the table. "It was right here."

I had no proof of voter fraud, of course. I'm not suggesting that. Neither of us was about to accuse anyone specific, no individual, like the guy sitting nearest. And maybe the ballot was just lost or misplaced. But it sure felt like a shifty little pickpocketing, although I would like to have believed it was unlikely. The missing ballot was somewhat unnerving, but it wasn't going to influence the outcome in any major way, like the fixed ballots in an election in Russia. And honestly, I no longer cared where my song ended up, how the crowd measured it against others. It no longer mattered, if it ever did. That may be hard to imagine for anyone who has ever entered a competition of any kind. There simply was no lingering envy. Accepting the missing ballot proved that to me. I was in a new place of acceptance. Maybe it was all the good karma of the night, or maybe it was the weed we had inhaled, but whatever it was, nothing was more important, more meaningful at that moment than the simple act of singing my song.

There were a number of standout songwriters in the second half, including a surprising performance from a woman who could have just as easily been the night manager at a McDonald's restaurant—a little overweight, a slightly worn-down appearance, clothes from a discount store, shoulder-length dirty-blonde hair permed into tight curls, evidence of long-ago teenage acne. My assessment of her appearance and what I anticipated from her performance certainly said more about me than her, but it's true, I never expected to hear what came from her skilled, callused fingers or to experience the level of honesty in her sweet but weathered voice. "Don't Mind Me" was voted the night's number three song, and it might have been my favorite.

"That was a killer song," I said, after seeking out the songwriter in the crowd of musicians standing near the bar after the winners had been announced.

"Thank you, I really appreciate that," she said timidly, her voice carrying a hint of a Virginia accent.

"She's the real deal," said a guitarist standing nearby. He had accompanied one of the night's earlier acts. "You should hear what else she's got."

I wished I could have.

Second place went to a local singer who had been out of the musical loop for a year or so. I had heard from someone that evening that she recently had a baby. "Waiting on the Stars" was a predictable country-favored ballad, but the songwriter was able to give it an alternative feel, enough to place. "Another Day" by Gene Mills was the top choice of the night. He had come in second place the year before and when his name was announced as the winner, the crowd erupted. Gene was a favorite from Richmond—a gray-bearded, guitar-playing, university philosophy professor whose academic discipline had clearly crept into the lyrics of his music, songs that sounded like the stylistic marriage of Townes Van Zandt and Alison Krauss. He sang "Another Day" with the ease and confidence that made it pretty clear to any doubter that Gene would be one of the night's winners.

It was silly to seriously consider that my song would get any real recognition. I won't deny that the possibility did enter my mind earlier in the process. But when the competition was over, I was thinking only of the songs and the songwriters I had watched and listened to and how just a handful had enough talent—that elusive, indefinable *something*—that boosted them above the others. I believed I was able to evoke sentiment in a song, but I was not a mover of mountains. I might have been able to excavate some flash of emotion with a musical phrase, but when it was all said and done, I was only a respectable amateur. And that was okay. When I played in those coffeehouses and the bars so many years ago, all I really wanted was to sing in the moment, to permit the vibrations of song and the authority of lyrics to deliver an immediate musical message, some sort of urgent truth to the world. That was all I could have hoped for or wanted that night in Rapunzel's. And if true, then I had something in common with great songwriters. In the late 1960s and early 1970s, the Troubadour in West Hollywood embraced the *song* and the song*writer*. Rapunzel's was the same. Both championed the music, not the act. Bob Dylan, Joni Mitchell, Neil Young, James Taylor, Tom Waits—the list goes on and on—offered their first musical narratives in the five-hundred-seat Troubadour, played their personal songs in the moment, for the moment. And like each of them in their purest form, I sang that night at Rapunzel's not because I had some fantasy of becoming a superstar, an opening act at a stadium concert, or was imagining the dream of making a record. No. I just wanted to sing my song, like the songwriters at the famous Troubadour who came to offer something fleeting, something visceral. A long time ago, I read somewhere that the only two jobs of a Zen monk are sitting and sweeping. The sitting is meditation and the sweeping, or raking, is the only other work in his world, and when he sweeps he concentrates on nothing else because at that instant there *is* nothing else. He senses every movement of the muscles in his hands, arms, and the beauty of this modest act in the moment he is executing it. It is his solitary state of mind. A Zen monk I am not and mindfulness is—at best—a continuous exercise in trying, but for me, playing my song on stage was my authentic attempt at a private act of sweeping.

* * *

It was nearly midnight, almost four hours of songs, singers, and judgment. And as the crew turned off the sound system and the stage lights, the regional music magnet known as Rapunzel's became a simple tavern in the Virginia hills. Friends gathered in clumps, holding bottles of beer and glasses of wine. Everyone was quicker to laugh. The adrenaline pumped into the room by the night's music had faded into a comfortable fatigue.

"And to think I was considering not coming," I said to Leslie, the two of us standing near the stage, observing the crowd.

"That was simply not an option," she said.

"Really?"

"I wasn't going to let that happen."

"Oh, you weren't, huh?"

Leslie tucked her arm into mine and gently bumped her hip against mine, accentuating her resolve.

Just then, off in the far corner, I saw the quick flash of a phone camera. Someone was taking pictures. Earlier in the evening, Leslie and I had asked a woman sitting nearby to snap a couple of photos as we cuddled together near the stage. During my performance, Leslie took a few more, and earlier in the day on our tour of wineries, Leslie had spotted an old barn. On an outside weather-beaten wall was a NO TRESPASSING sign, bleached by the Virginia sun. "That would be a great place for a photo of you and your guitar," she said, as we turned the tight corner in the narrow road that led to a tucked-away vineyard. I liked the setting, but I wondered if the sign was a statement from the musical gods. *Was I supposed to be here?* "We have to stop there on the way back. That would be a really good spot," Leslie said. "We're taking that photo."

Another phone camera flashed inside Rapunzel's.

"I really like that picture of us near the stage," Leslie said, recalling the photo taken earlier.

"*You* look great. *I* look like your dad," I said.

Leslie's youthfulness is unmistakable. She appears to have lived only thirty-five of her fifty-two years. Her eyes illuminate. She smiles often. The hair that falls around her face appears to have come from an earlier decade, and yoga and a commitment to eating as many green things as possible have certainly fueled her energy. Her clash with cancer had changed everything, and it showed.

"Oh, no. I think you look great," she insisted.

"I'm old."

Leslie didn't like when I said that. And I said it often. I frequently joked about my family DNA and how few of my ancestors had lived past the age of seventy-six. There was the prostate cancer that metastasized and killed my father. Heart and lung problems after miraculously surviving 1950's tuberculosis finally got my mother. There were smokers and drinkers, too. But it was the biological marriage of one set of genes interacting with another set of genes that had at least partially set my fate. This is what I believed, or at least what I had talked myself in to.

"But you really like the one at the barn?" I asked.

On the way out of the vineyard's valley earlier in the day, we had pulled the car off the narrow road to a patch of gravel. Leaning my back against the side of the barn, I held the guitar against my chest, resting it partially on a bended knee and pretended to be playing. The angle of the late afternoon sun forced me to look down toward my boots, not at the camera. Leslie loved what she saw, convinced that what was being captured was worthy of album cover art.

"I love that photo," Leslie said. "It's perfect."

Years ago in a fit to simplify my life, at a time when I believed I needed to cleanse my existence of the unnecessary, I donated bags of old clothes, tossed out an unworkable lawnmower, an old clock radio, chipped plates and mugs, and charred and dented pots and pans. There were boxes of decades-old files and documents that no longer held meaning or significance, golf clubs I never used, a pair of cross-country skis that could find better use with someone else. And there were all those vinyl albums. This act of ridding my life of these records now seems terribly misguided, but the move came years before vinyl's resurgence, the hipster's fashion statement. Now, I could probably make a few dollars selling them. Or I could have kept them, at least the better ones. Those old album covers, along with the music on grooved plastic, were touchstones. They represented stages of my musical progression, my personal evolution. Inside one of a half-dozen milk crates was The Monkees' first album with a photo of Davy Jones, Peter Tork, Michael Nesmith, and Micky Dolenz leaning on each other, fresh faces smiling at the camera. I had The Who's *Who's Next* album with the defiant front cover photo of the four band members peeing on a wall. The art on Led Zeppelin's *Houses of the Holy* was weird, nearly spooky, but still cool with its image of naked golden-haired children crawling on an enhanced photo of Northern Ireland's Giant's Causeway. And I had a copy of *Abbey Road*, with the most iconic album cover photo in history.

"It's good. You have a good eye for pictures, girl," I said. "The barn photo looks like it could be the front of a country music album."

Digital images are instantaneous. We can judge them in the moment. I'm certain Leslie deleted a few of the barn photos before choosing the best of the bunch. But I wonder where the dozens and dozens of original film images of all those iconic album covers are today. Someone has them. Locked away in a darkroom somewhere, a bank vault. I wonder how many were taken and rejected before selecting the single picture that burns in our musical memories. And I wonder if there are rolls of film from those photo shoots stashed away somewhere that have never been developed, flashes of imperfection and missteps yet unrevealed, or hidden gems lost in photographic time. Unlike film, digital photos do not permit shortcomings, blemishes, or flaws to remain secrets, or do they allow for the undiscovered prize. We know instantly when we have a keeper, and we rarely hesitate to immediately delete the undesirable.

All the instantly developed memories of that night in Virginia—the ones we really wanted to keep—would be filed safely away, like all of the modern-day digital images found on phones and computers. But as we said goodbye to Rapunzel's and carried ourselves and my old guitar out the door, I could only wonder if in the darkrooms of our minds there might be rolls of analog film that someday could be discovered and carefully, lovingly developed to expose treasures unknown.

Chapter 10

I can recall the flavors of the Sunday lunch at the winery—tart, savory, nutty, sweet. But Leslie remembered details.

"There was chorizo, and a special blue cheese. Olives were great. Almonds. I believe they were Marcona almonds? And there was that date and brown butter jam," she said. "So good."

It was tapas, a potpourri of bite sizes. We sat at a high table in the early afternoon sun on the patio at Pippin Hill and ordered a bottle of cabernet franc, 2013. Wildflowers grew on the knoll behind me and off to the right, ornamental vineyards framed the winery's long, winding entranceway road. It was a stunning day, ridiculously idyllic, warm and bright, and we were rested, sleeping a bit longer that morning after the night at Rapunzel's. We waited a few minutes for one of the few outside tables. It was a chance to soak up a little more of the benefits of central Virginia, to enjoy the remains of the night before, and as it turned out, to permit my unconscious mind to prepare for the question I had not planned to ask, but would ask anyway.

"So," I said, seated at our table, my eyes hiding behind dark aviator sunglasses. "What do you think it would be like if we lived together?" The query sort of sprouted like a wild bean.

Leslie smiled nervously. "Oh, my," she said, and reached for her wineglass.

"You can't tell me you haven't thought about this," I said, trying to recover from the surprise of actually asking the question.

"Sure, yes of course. I've thought about it," she answered.

"I don't want to force you into this conversation. But, you know, it's been on my mind and, well, it's a beautiful day," I said, pouring more wine into my glass. The topic was out there now; no turning back.

"Okay. Yeah," Leslie said, vocally steadying herself. "And

you'd come to my place?" she asked.

"Well, what do you think? Makes more sense, doesn't it?"

Leslie took a sip from her glass and then exhaled. "Wow," she sighed, looking past me toward the mountains. "We are really talking about this."

"We don't have to," I said.

"No. No. It's good," she said, inhaling deeply. "We'd have to wait until my niece leaves, of course." Leslie's niece lived with her and planned to stay until her summer wedding.

"And there's your son," I said. "I don't want to be *that* guy."

Leslie's daughter was an elementary teacher in Iowa and had her own place, had established a life, but her son was scheduled to graduate from college in the spring and his plans were unclear. The house was cozy but small and I wasn't about to be the man who moved in with his mother and left him homeless. He had dibs.

"I think he'll end up at his dad's until he finds something of his own," Leslie said. "Makes more sense." She then looked past me toward the wildflowers and settled deep into her chair.

I emptied what remained of the bottle of wine into Leslie's glass. "You okay?" I asked.

"Maybe we should get another bottle of wine," she joked.

"Babe, we can wait on this discussion," I suggested, feeling as if I may have jumped the starting line.

"No. It's good," Leslie said, reaching across the table to hold my hand. "I just didn't expect this, you know, right now. Today. Here."

I raised my glass and surveyed our view. "What better time and place?"

She elevated her glass to tap mine, clinking the tops and bottoms, a good luck ritual we had adopted. "You know," she thought aloud. "We can do this. *I* can do this."

"We have time to think through the particulars," I said. "But there is absolutely no rush. It's just something I've been thinking about, you know?"

Leslie had experienced two long relationships that were not good ones. Men she lived with had turned her world upside down. What would a third one be like?

"It's all good. Really," she said. "It's actually very good."

I leaned across the table to kiss her, then whispered, "I love you, Leslie O'Hare."

"I love you, David W. Berner, but remember, *you* brought it up." She laughed and sipped from her glass.

Just then the waiter returned, "Need anything?" he asked.

"We're good," Leslie answered. She then looked toward me. "We are wonderful."

* * *

You can be sixteen or you can be fifty-seven and it just doesn't matter. Talking with someone about commitment on any level is always intimidating. And then believing that you can actually follow through is even scarier. It could be deciding to live together or as monumental as agreeing to marry, or it could be simply and innocently asking someone on a first date for coffee or lunch. No matter, it's all the same. I felt relatively confident about the conversation at the winery, bringing up the subject, but like a first date, you're walking the plank, standing at the edge of the deep end. The reason for this anxiety, I think, is quite simple. You cannot predict the future. None of us knows what is really going to happen. The only thing that is assured is that we will grow old, and that means the unknown and the fear of failure are going to stick to us like leeches.

We all remember our first real date and the other firsts that came afterward. They are tattooed on us. That sensation of walking a tightrope without a net is palpable and always will be. The anxiety of how the two of you will get along is heightened to ridiculous degrees, and then there are the outside forces and factors, all the things that could go wrong, adding to the fragility of promise.

As a young teen, I hung out at my first real girlfriend's house on Saturday afternoons and we occasionally stopped for an ice cream or a Coke after school, but then came the real thing. It was just the two of us with no parental supervision, going out for the night like grownups. My father dropped us off in the city and we walked across the bridge to see Alice Cooper and Three Dog Night at Pittsburgh's Three Rivers Stadium, a venue that a few years later would be demolished. At least it lasted longer than the relationship. Both were doomed anyway. The old baseball stadium was an unremarkable concrete bowl with no character and no soul. The girl was pretty. She had deep-set blue eyes, shoulder-length brown hair, and a long and lean body, standing about three inches taller than me. Overall, the night went rather smoothly, no outside forces to derail the evening. But we were young. It was eighth grade. This wasn't going to last, endure in any possible way. The only thing that really mattered that night was that I wouldn't do something stupid, wouldn't stumble over what would surely be an awkward kiss, and in the end she would somehow, someway still like me.

It was many years later when I vividly recalled that first date. I had received a panicky phone call from my fifteen-year-old son who had been out on his very first night alone with a girl.

"Dad," Graham whispered. I could hear his hand rubbing against the phone, shielding the mouthpiece. "I don't have enough money."

Graham's older brother, Casey, had just graduated from high school and had been to homecoming and prom, and somehow had handled the inevitable awkwardness and mishaps of those early girl-boy experiences. He had navigated his way through holding hands, the kiss goodnight, and the self-conscious dance of paying for a night out with a girl. It was now Graham's turn.

The girl had worn an overly formal pink dress with ruffles

around the waist and a knee-length hem. There was glitter in her eye shadow and shiny crimson lipstick drawn unevenly on her mouth. Graham knew she loved the Olive Garden, so that's where he wanted to take her to celebrate her birthday.

"The bill is over fifty dollars," Graham whispered.

"What?" I blurted.

"She ordered two appetizers, a salad, Fettuccine Alfredo, some other pasta thing, chocolate cake. She just kept eating." Graham was in a stall in the restaurant's bathroom. It was the only private place he could find.

"Okay, look," I said. "I'll come by and give you some money. But it's going to take a little time to get there."

I couldn't help to think about the Olive Garden's menu, the two-for-one specials, and something the restaurant chain called its "Endless Salad Bowl."

"Graham, how the hell do you spend fifty bucks at Olive Garden?"

"I don't know," Graham said. "She just kept knocking it down. But I didn't want to seem cheap, like some loser. I like her, Dad."

An outside factor had threatened to spoil the night.

I pulled into the parking lot and waited, my eyes fixed on the restaurant's front door. Families and couples came and went. Then I saw Graham. His eyes quickly searched the parking lot. I honked the horn and Graham ran to the car. I handed him ten dollars through the window.

"Don't forget the tip," I reminded him.

Graham disappeared through the doorway.

I rested my neck against the driver's headrest and remembered my first date,

how Alice Cooper had belted out "Eighteen" into the night and how I was certain everything in my entire world would be wonderful if I could just get through the evening without her hating me.

As Graham came through the restaurant's door, the sun was

painting a thin red line across the horizon. It was the kind of balmy night that had me wishing for a convertible or a big front porch where I could sleep in a chaise lounge until morning. As they walked toward the car, I could see broad smiles on both Graham and his girl, a sure sign that no matter the forces that might have ruined the night, she still liked him and all had been rescued.

* * *

As Leslie and I stepped away from our table at Pippin Hill, we held each other's hands and looked out over the wildflowers one last time.

"I'm taking this with me," she said, grabbing our empty wine bottle from the table and stuffing it inside her purse. "It's my souvenir. *Our* souvenir."

Unknowns were before us, so much only time would answer. We had roads to travel, rivers to cross. Forces unseen might someday knock us off balance. But on that afternoon, so much appeared certain. Clearly, the lunch at Pippin had not been our first date and we were no longer kids, but nonetheless it had been a milestone, just like a first date, complete with that splendid combination of innocent apprehension and uneasy exhilaration that comes only from taking a risk. Decades ago, in the quiet minutes alone after saying goodnight to the girl I had taken to see Alice Cooper, I realized that she honestly, amazingly still liked me. And on that afternoon in Virginia while walking from Pippen's patio to the car, I realized that the girl now by my side, the one holding my hand, also amazingly still liked me. Maybe, like my son's night at the Olive Garden restaurant, it was time to be rescued.

"You okay to drive for a while?" Leslie asked.

"I am good to do just about anything," I said, as she tossed me the car keys.

The number of visitors to the winery had grown over the last hour or so; families, children, and double dates filled the grounds. It now belonged to the usual lively Sunday crowd. Pippin Hill was no longer ours. Virginia was no longer ours.

Chapter 11

I got sucked up in one of those Facebook questionnaires. It was the one that asked what 1960s band you'd be if you could be a 1960s band. First time I answered the questions, I was The Beatles. Second time it was Pink Floyd. Third time it was The Doors. Different moods at different times produced different answers. One of the questions in the survey was "What's your hobby?" and one of the choices was "smoking pot." I don't think I chose that answer, but I can't be sure. Smoking pot is not a "hobby" of mine, but the other choices were just too dumb to select. Another question asked me to choose a particular object — a book, a guitar, sunglasses . . . or a *joint*. Well, I guess it is a band from the 1960s, right? The questionnaire also asked if I would like to get married and if I was a religious guy — tough questions for me. Then, the test asked me to pick one of four items: alcohol, coke, jellybeans, or hash. I'm assuming "coke" was really "Coke" — as in the soft drink — but maybe not. But hash was hash. Dope again. I'm convinced the more you selected the marijuana answers the more likely you got Pink Floyd as the band that most identified with your personality.

I bring this up because in the early going on the drive back to Chicago with Leslie at the wheel, I was running through another Facebook questionnaire on my phone, a way to kill some time. This questionnaire claimed it would answer: *What's your old person's name?* The very first enquiry: *When do you usually eat dinner?*

I looked up from my phone and asked Leslie, "You getting hungry at all?"

"Still full from the lunch at Pippin," she answered. "You *honestly* hungry?"

"I could eat," I said.

It was only 4:00 pm, dinnertime for old people.

Other questions on the old person's name test: *The neighbors are having a loud party, what do you do? Do you like cats? You're heading out for a party, what do you take with you?* One of the answers: *pepper spray. What do you like to drink?* Metamucil was not on the list. Finally, I was asked to pick a tchotchke. *None* was not one of the choices, so I selected the ceramic dog.

"You ever do these Facebook quizzes?" I asked Leslie.

"Which one?" she asked.

"It picks your old person's name."

"And?"

"Harold."

"Wow."

Harold—the guy who smokes a lot of dope and loves Pink Floyd. That Harold. Harold—the burnout with an original vinyl copy of *Dark Side of the Moon.*

"You okay driving a bit more?" I asked Leslie. "Steelers game is coming on. I'd love to listen, if I can, maybe online or pick it up on the radio as we move along here."

"You can't drive and listen at the same time?" Leslie smirked.

"You know me and football. We'd crash."

It was an insanely good day for the Steelers. Ben Roethlisberger threw for 500 yards, breaking records left and right. I was texting and calling my sons while tuning in radio stations and following the plays on the ESPN app on my phone. At one point, I yelped at a particularly spectacular play and scared the hell out of Leslie. She slammed on the brakes.

"What's wrong?" she cried.

"Oh, so sorry. Just a great pass," I explained.

Leslie playfully rolled her eyes.

Time passed quickly that afternoon—the game, the sunshine, the company, a little music—all of it helped ease away the hours on the road.

"What do you think about taking it all the way home?" Leslie asked, still at the wheel.

"It'll be midnight, maybe after. Not sure I want to do that."

"Okay, let's book a place. Something cheap."

After gassing up and a switch at the driver seat, Leslie searched her phone and found a Days Inn outside Dayton. Before checking in, we headed to a local Max & Erma's to get a bite.

A slutty cop greeted us at the door and a cowboy waited on us.

"Why on Halloween do bars insist on making their employees dress up like idiots?" I asked.

"Not a Halloween fan?" Leslie already knew the answer.

"Stupid."

An adult in costume is a ridiculous ritual, even creepy. People pretending they are something they are not, secretly wishing to be a vampire, Harry Potter, or SpongeBob SquarePants. I saw a grown man dressed like the yellow cartoon character walking through my neighborhood one Halloween night. Tell me, *that's* not creepy? Add my dislike of this bizarre holiday with the weight of a long day. I was far more exhausted than I had expected, despite doing little of the driving and feeling as if we had made great travel time. It seemed as if the real world was sneaking back into my life. The weekend of wine and song, love and new promises had faded behind the realities of a monotonous drive. The Facebook questions were fun and the Steelers game was magnificent. But now it was a greasy chicken sandwich, soggy fries, cold nachos, and the worst motel of the trip.

"Does that sign say something about NASCAR?" Leslie asked, as we pulled the car up to the entranceway of the Days Inn parking lot.

"Big enough sign?" I wondered. The banner covered nearly the entire front door archway from one end of the entrance to the other.

"They give discounts to pace car drivers?" Leslie asked.

"That's what it says. You got your pace car ID card handy?

Maybe we can get a break."

The tiny lobby allowed for barely enough room for us to stand. Behind the crowded counter was a round-faced woman in her late twenties, pointedly explaining the night's duties to a wide-eyed young man.

"After you punch this, you have to get them to sign this," she said, handing him a document of some kind. "And don't forget to get the license plate number." She turned toward me and smiled. "Be right with you, honey."

The young man stiffened. He was frozen like a squirrel in the middle of the road.

"But, how do I . . . ?" he stammered.

"Don't worry about that," the woman ordered. She threw her purse over her shoulder and grabbed a set of car keys. "Lock the back door. No one gets a key to the restrooms if they're not a guest." She slipped quickly past the young man and moved to the front of the counter. "It'll all be fine. No worries. All good."

The young man—apparently a brand-new employee—was now staring at the small computer screen on the counter. "But—"

"I'm out of here," the woman said, standing only briefly near the door. "He'll get you all settled in," she said to Leslie. "He's cool." Then she lifted her car keys above her head, shook them and yelled out, "Bye, bye and goodnight, ya'll!" And she was gone.

The young man looked up at me then glanced again at the computer screen and back at me.

"Hi," he said softly.

"Yeah, hello," I said, speaking slowly. "We have a reservation." I was not confidant that there would actually be a record of this or that this poor guy would know how to find it.

"Okay," he said, shuffling papers, tapping the computer keyboard, and then looking up again at me. "It's for tonight, right?"

"Uh, huh," I said. *Patience is a virtue,* my mother used to say.

Fifteen minutes later, we had the room key, actually one of those key cards.

The Days Inn's architecture had that serial killer vibe about it, a setting you'd see in a slasher film—two floors, wrought iron railings that hadn't been painted in years, the rooms' dirty brown doors faced the highway, the *D* in the motel sign flickered off and on, and all of this sat under the dim, yellow haze of overhead security lights.

We entered the room cautiously.

"The lock is broken," I said, trying to close the door behind us. There was no way to fully bolt the door from the inside. I tilted a chair and leaned it tight against the knob, like people in the movies do when they're frantically trying to keep the zombies from getting them inside their home.

"This place is probably the worst we could have found," Leslie said, cautiously looking around at the polyester floral bedspreads, the two white drinking cups wrapped in clear protective plastic on the nightstand between the two queen beds, and the overly large television remote with two of its buttons missing.

"Not going to get the Ritz for fifty-nine dollars."

"This light doesn't work," Leslie said, repeatedly flicking the metal switch of the bedside lamp.

"No bulb," I said, examining the light through the top of the dusty shade.

"Well, it's just one night. Still, would you mind taking the bed near the door," Leslie said. "That way the murderer will get you first."

It was the least I could do.

Leslie washed up and sat at the small rickety desk in her T-shirt and panties, drinking red wine from a Styrofoam cup, and working through emails. At least the Wi-Fi worked. I was in sweats on the bed browsing Facebook. Over the last few days, little else but the songwriting contest and the two of us had been on our minds. We had been immersed, saturated in the weekend and now were being tugged back onto life's treadmill, little by little. Virginia was five hundred miles behind us; the night at Rapunzel's had faded in to the two-dozen hours we had left behind.

"In the spirit of full disclosure," I said. "There's a response here on a post from the weekend. It's Laura."

"No!" Leslie said, turning in her chair to face me.

"Yeah. It's a reaction to one of the photos at the winery. You and me."

"She's stalking you."

I can think of only one of my past relationships since my marriage ended that concluded badly. The rest simply fizzled or came to an amicable conclusion, pretty tame. Some of the women have remained friends. Not drinking, football, or let's-go-have-dinner buddies, but, at the very least, Facebook acquaintances.

"She's not stalking me," I snarled. "Come on."

"Oh, she's stalking. Trust me. What'd she say?"

"*Looks like you found someone special in your life.* Then she "liked" the photo."

"Oh geez. Which photo is it?"

"Our backs are to the vineyards. Mountains. The one where I have the sunglasses on."

"They just keep popping up, don't they? How many are out there again?"

I don't think Leslie wanted to hear me count them out. We had talked about all this before and she knew the stories, at least the Cliff Notes versions. She simply didn't particularly enjoy living her life—and our life together—among the accumulated boxes of my past lives.

"It's all over, Les. You know that, right?"

"Oh, I know that," she said, smiling. "But the women, they're like little patches of snow in spring that just won't melt."

I closed my computer and set it on the wobbly nightstand. "Let's call it a night. We want to get going early."

Leslie turned off the desk lamp. I re-secured the chair against the door and peeped out the grimy window to see the flickering, shadowy lights of the food-fast restaurants and gas stations. Dayton was quiet. Leslie put in her earplugs, I set the alarm on my phone, we kissed goodnight, she in her bed and me in the other—the one nearest the barricaded door, as we agreed, so the murderer would get me first.

"You know I'm not mad, right?" Leslie whispered in the darkness.

"I know, babe," I whispered back.

* * *

Individually plastic-wrapped bagels, paper towels for napkins, muddy coffee, a first-generation microwave, all cramped inside a room of white plastic tables and chairs, and from the small wall-mounted TV, the bark of Fox News.

"Obama doesn't get it!" the commentator snapped. She was blonde, wore a tight red dress, and gestured emphatically. "His immigration policy will destroy America."

A man—maybe in his forties and dressed in an untucked light blue shirt and Carhartt khakis—drank orange juice and stared at the television. I guessed he might have been a truck driver. A young couple sat in the corner, silent and sullen, and an older man with a comb-over balanced two paper plates in one hand and black coffee in a paper cup in the other.

"Looks like a hearty breakfast," I said.

"Orders from the wife," the man said. "You know how that goes."

"Breakfast in bed," Leslie quipped.

"Keeping her happy is half of the battle," he smiled, rolled his eyes, and moved through the glass door that led to the outside walkway to the rooms.

"I don't think Obama likes this country," another Fox commentator growled. She was now on the right side of the TV's split screen from a remote location somewhere. She, too, was blonde. "Obama doesn't get it and letting immigrants just roam across the border is simply dangerous."

"Too bad we don't have the remote," Leslie said.

I leaned in. "I think if we tried to change the channel there'd be a riot."

"Look at what they are doing to our America!" the first commentator scowled.

* * *

I was at the wheel this time as we drove out of the Days Inn parking lot, a coffee cup in the drink holder. The morning was grayer than the others on our trip. The sun shone but it was filtered, like the light of a street lantern in fog. We kept it quiet in the car. No radio, no music, little talk. We were both a little weary. It wasn't long before Indiana—flat and stark—took over the landscape.

In the distance, north of I-70, an old tractor rusted in a soybean field.

"I feel like we should be listening to John Mellencamp," Leslie said, watching the wide-open farms roll by from the passenger-side window.

"It's kind of sad out here," I said.

After a moment, Leslie turned to me. "But you know what I'm doing instead?" she asked. "I'm still singing your song in my head."

It was at that very moment that I no longer thought of my music—the song I played at Rapunzel's—as mine. It had gone somewhere else, traveled somewhere new, and belonged to someone else.

Chapter 12

Months after the Virginia trip, I was bent over the examination table in my doctor's office, my pants and underwear to my knees.

"You're going to feel like you need to urinate," the doctor said. I heard the snap of a latex glove being stretched onto his right hand just before he put his finger up my butt.

"Oh," I whimpered.

"Does it hurt?" he asked.

"No. Just got to pee."

He removed his finger and took off the glove.

"Feels normal for a man of your age," he said, washing his hands in the small stainless steel sink.

"Of my age?" I asked.

"Prostates get bigger as we get older."

"So I have an enlarged prostate?"

The doctor dried his hands with a paper towel.

"I wouldn't say that," he said. "Normal stuff. But we'll still do the test."

Since Dad died of advanced prostate cancer, I had had the PSA test done yearly, the prostate-specific antigen test. But then I switched healthcare plans. Time passed. I missed a few years.

"How's your stream?" the doctor asked.

"Stream?"

"Do you pee like an old man?"

I looked puzzled.

"Does it come out in a nice stream, or does it dribble?"

"Oh," I said. I thought for a moment. "It streams pretty good, I guess."

This was now officially an old man's doctor appointment. Prostate talk is right up there with going to the discounted matinee movie, having dinner at 4:30 in the afternoon, and reading the obituary page in the newspaper.

"And do you get up in the middle of the night to urinate?" the doctor asked.

"Now and then."

"Well, you are fifty-seven," he said. "We'll get the numbers and take a look. What age was your father?"

"Late sixties when he was first diagnosed," I said.

"Okay, good to know."

I followed a nurse down the hall into a small room with two chairs pushed against the wall. They looked like chairs from a high school class, hard plastic with the small arm-desk connected to the left side. Another nurse wrapped a thick piece of rubber around my arm and tightened it. She warned me about the prick of the needle and withdrew two vials of blood.

"All set," she said. "The doctor will call you."

* * *

Days later, I was inside a Starbucks just outside of Chicago, sitting at a small table trying to finish the words to a new song. It was to be a gift for Leslie. To my back a trio of boys talked about their budding rock 'n' roll band.

"Dude, I'm gonna get naked on stage." One teenager said. "You know that's gonna happen, man. I'm gonna do it!"

"You're the artist, man," another insisted. "I defer to you, dude."

"I'm writing some great shit right now, man," said the artist.

"I think we need some social media," another said.

"It can't just be a fucking Facebook page," the artist asserted. "Instagram, that's the shit."

"I know this guy who can video us," one of them added.

"That's when I get naked, dude!"

I played a coffeehouse on a college campus dressed in shorts and a T-shirt once. That was as close to naked as I ever was on stage. It was sometime during the beginning of the Punk era, if I remember it correctly. Bands were doing edgy stuff. The sensitive singer-songwriter vibe was fading. It was Johnny Rotten time, you might say. Some girl at my college radio station was into that stuff. She conducted some interviews for the station and when The J. Geils Band came to Clarion State College one spring semester she got access backstage before the show.

"Why do you guys throw up on stage?"

I heard the tape, so I know this is exactly what she asked J. Geils, the band's front man. I'm pretty sure he told her to "fuck off."

J. Geils did not throw up on stage. No one in the band voluntarily puked during a concert. This was a *rock* band, not a punk band. And if I remember, punk bands didn't necessarily throw up on stage either. They just smashed guitars or started stage riots. The girl had clearly mixed her genres or she was high. The point is: I was never into the shock era. So, hearing the "artist" sitting behind me at Starbucks announce his intentions only made me smile. For this kid, the art of music was at least partially the shock value, seeing what social norm could be rattled. It is part of rock's raw, rebellious roots and I'm all for that. Still, I needed the *music* to capture me first, then maybe I could accept the naked guitarist or a singer's vomit. Elvis had to have something good to sing before he shook his hips, right? However, I was certain the song I was trying to write that afternoon would never be performed in the buff or with a bucket by my side.

I hadn't written any music since "Under the Moon"—the song that failed to make the cut for the song contest. In fact, I hadn't played the guitar much since returning from Virginia. But Valentine's Day was a few days away. Leslie and I had decided not to exchange gifts or cards, but maybe I could offer a song, one for me as much as for her. I had a bit of the music figured out—a chord structure and a melody that took me weeks to smooth out—but I wrestled with the words. Simple or complex? Deep or sweet? Rhymes or no rhymes?

Before playing coffeehouses and small bars when I was young, I was in a four-piece band. We formed the band in high school and kept it going while in college. We called ourselves Seaport. So very lame, when I think of it now. Not sure where the name came from, but we knew we wanted a one-word band. We came of age in a one-word era—Chicago, America, Argent. Does anyone remember Argent? "Hold Your Head Up" was the band's only real hit. It sold over a million copies. Seaport was just a bar band but we did all right. We made a little money playing weekends and we had fun, but we never played original music. Never wrote a song as a band. Writing songs came later, in college, alone in a dorm room with my acoustic, the same guitar that went with me to Virginia, the old Yamaha. The process was singular and introspective. Although, I remember one song written over a weekend inside a cabin in Cook Forest in the Allegheny Mountains of Pennsylvania with a bunch of college buddies. "Smokewood Country" was a collaborative effort, a country-flavored ode to nature, and it was hideous. But if I asked those old friends if they remembered the song, I'm certain each of them probably could sing some of it. I wrote a song about my college girlfriend, too. "She's the One" was composed when we were breaking up. It was a desperate attempt to keep her, and it failed. I don't remember one chord or one line of that song. I think it was in the key of D. That's about all I can recall. There were other songs and I remember little bits of those. But others have vanished. For decades after college, I wrote nothing. And now, I was trying to keep it going in some little way, gasping musically, wrestling to write more, to be disciplined, to find the muse, the inspiration, and the guts to say something in a song.

My son Graham started writing songs when he was a teenager. He had been in and out of metal bands for a couple of years. He wrote the lyrics and vocalized. Metal musicians don't call it singing, because it's not. It's a guttural scream, a raspy cry, a deep throaty shriek. It's rough stuff, dark material. But that's metal and that's Graham and that's okay. It's truthful and it's honest. As far as I know, my older son Casey has never written a song; however, during his middle school years when he played saxophone, he could blow out a pretty good version of "Tequila"—the iconic sax song from pop radio, and sometimes he embellished the melody a bit. His way of composing, I suppose. When the two of them were in middle school, I took them to their first concert—Crosby, Stills and Nash. I told them to pay attention to the lyrics and the harmonies. But I think Casey was more interested in the old hippies and the dope in the air. Graham, on the other hand, liked David Crosby. "He's the one that writes the weird stuff, right?" Graham said, during the show's intermission. Who else could have written "Déjà Vu," the best song about paranoia ever penned? Casey apparently didn't leave the concert uninfluenced. The music that night and all the other songs I would introduce him to helped him crush the competition in a game of Name That Tune while listening to the radio during a college spring break road trip. He texted me from somewhere in Nebraska: *I'm winning because of you!* Casey has moved on to his own music, but I like to think I set the foundation. And that's what I was relying on while trying to write lyrics at the Starbucks that afternoon—my foundation— songs that rang true for me, a mix of old and new styles, words that were meaningful, at least to me.

I had plenty of work to do.

* * *

That night I drew a bath and placed a burning candle in a glass holder on the edge of the old porcelain tub in my apartment and grabbed three books. The first few pages of Denis Johnson's *Tree of Smoke* contain some of the best writing I've read anywhere, at any time. Dense, real, raw, and it captures the absurdity and personal damages of the Vietnam War in just eight hundred words. *Doghouse Roses* is musician Steve Earle's book of short stories. I cherished this copy for a couple of reasons. Earle was a hero of mine, a killer singer-songwriter. But more than that, Earle had personally autographed my copy. Leslie knew someone back in Iowa City who worked inside the art community and when Earle came to play the town, her friend was helping to coordinate his needs. Leslie worked her magic, got the book in front of Earle, and he signed it. The third was Joan Didion's collection of essays: *The White Album*. The essay from which the title comes is the best reflection on the end of the 1960's peace and love generation ever composed.

I turned off my phone, turned off the brightest of the bathroom lights, tested the water with my hands, added some cold to modify the heat, and settled in.

Valentine's Day was coming and I could not find a way to complete the song. I had been feeling emotionally off balance and was unsure of what triggered the malaise—unrelenting frigid February weather, a recent minor falling out with an old friend that I won't get into here, or maybe I simply needed a diversion. Since coming home from Virginia, I had been consumed with my college classes that I'd been assigned to teach, and the holidays came and there had been all that juggling of people and emotions. Leslie believed I needed more exercise. Then there was that prostate test.

I rolled the pages of Didion's book over its spine so I could hold it with one hand and began to read.

In "The White Album" essay, Didion chronicles her own personal anxiety during the last years of 1960s and early 1970s—Robert Kennedy's assassination, the Manson murders, the trial of Black Panther Huey Newton, the studio work of The Doors as Jim Morrison slipped into madness. She tries to make sense of it. As I navigated through dog-eared pages and the old notes I had written in the margins, I was finding newness in the words. I wouldn't call it an epiphany but it was something fresh and relevant, something I had not quite experienced from those words before.

Bathwater dripped from my hands and the book's pages soaked up the room's humidity.

Between the words and lines of that essay may have been the beginning of an explanation for my recent angst. Didion struggles to understand the 1960s, but she fails. She appears to come to the conclusion that the acts, the incidents, the people are all too random to allow for any clear narrative of the times. And *that* is exactly the point. Maybe there is no meaning to what happens to us, around us; maybe there is no point to anything. It's simply accidental, arbitrary. In the search for meaning—deep or superficial—we lose our way. Not everything needs an explanation or deserves it, and in the challenge to clarify we fall off balance. Especially as we get older, we seem to want to control things and maybe because of that we go adrift. Like Didion, we experience anxiety, worry, bouts of some level of depression and struggle as we try to find the answers to why things are as they are, discover our narrative, our larger story. Maybe there is no story. I was on a big emotional high just before, during, and immediately after Virginia, then life and all its haphazardness seeped in and instead of embracing it, I tried to regulate it, understand it. That may have been the natural progression of things. But in that process I had misplaced my thankfulness for the opportunity to play in the competition, for being recognized, for having those lovely days with Leslie on the road. I was navel-gazing, trying to comprehend and adjust instead of allowing life to just happen. Let it go. Let it be. Didion had tried to make sense of her time, but in the end, relinquishing control, giving up trying to figure it all out helped her to make things clear.

I leaned back against the tub's rear edge and sighed, soaking for a minute in what had become lukewarm conditions. Then, at the moment a delicate chill began to surround me, I turned the hot water knob and let it run full open to slowly re-warm the tub water and return me to that comfort I was looking for. It was the one thing I could control — the temperature of the bathwater.

* * *

Dusk had just fallen and snow had sprinkled a white dusting on the top of Leslie's black wool cap as we stood in the growing line of concertgoers outside the Tivoli Theatre. It was just past 6:00 pm — the scheduled time for the doors to open — but the entrance had yet to be unlocked and the evening's chill was quickly becoming a bitter wind. The Guinness and the nachos and potato skin appetizers at the Irish Pub had fueled us against the punishment of the season, but the deteriorating weather was now powering my impatience.

"See anyone moving up there?" I asked Leslie, as she peered around the edge of the line toward the front entrance.

"Oh, here we go. Someone's moving."

"Thank god."

Leslie moved to the curb off the sidewalk to get a better look. "False alarm. Just people huddling together."

I pulled my barn jacket — a heavy cotton garment with too little protection for this kind of night — around my shoulders and fastened the last button at the collar. "And the concert starts at seven?"

Leslie nodded and rubbed my arm. It was clear she had been aware of the unevenness that had been recently swirling around me and had reminded me to live in the present, to be mindful, to be grateful. She was patient and she was right. I had no business slipping into discontent.

But there was not room for that now. There was a concert to attend.

The Tivoli is a grand old place — restored French Renaissance style with a shallow stage and great acoustics. Several rows of front seats were roped off for VIPs, but we were able to get close, just behind the reserved area. Dawes—the band from Los Angeles, the band Leslie and I believed only young people knew about—was the opener, but it was clear half the crowd had come to see them not the headliner, The Jayhawks—the band from Minnesota. Taylor Goldsmith plays guitar and writes the songs for Dawes.

"He looks a little like Ben Stiller," Leslie whispered, as the crowd rose to its feet to belt out the chorus to "When My Time Comes"—a song some have said is about the inevitability of death. But that's a light interpretation. I always thought it was about the artistic experience, living life to gain material for writing, for offering art, growing old enough to give art—his music—weight.

I didn't want Goldsmith to look like Ben Stiller. It didn't fit the image of a masterful songwriter. But he did; he looked a great deal like Ben Stiller.

Who did I look like on stage in Virginia? The old Billy Joel? The old Peter Gabriel?

Leslie wrapped her fingers into mine and we sang the chorus with a thousand other voices in the warmth of the old theatre.

What everyone was waiting to hear was the song that attempts to tackle the unending question of the meaning of life. It's a lofty, almost pretentious subject to take on. But Goldsmith didn't appear to be trying to actually answer that unsolvable inquiry; he was only helping us to interpret the question.

The first chord ignited a roar from the seats.

"I'm going to try not to cry," Leslie said, biting her lip.

I wasn't about to understand how I might react to hearing this song. I'd often cried while playing it over the speakers in my car.

"A Little Bit of Everything" has three verses, scenes really. The first is the story of a young man about to jump from the Golden Gate Bridge. "Why are you doing this?" a police officer asks. In the second, an old man, coming to terms with a life of regret and sadness, decides he deserves more. And in the final, a groom convinces his bride that their wedding is more than a ceremony and that their love is beyond some "stupid little ring." Instead, their love is the sum of *a little bit of everything,* the same things that led the old man to consider more than the tragedies in his life and the young man to consider hope when seemingly all is lost. Leslie and I stood at our seats and slowly swayed to the melody, softly joining in the lovely ache of the song's final lines.

It's not some message written in the dark,
Or some truth that's no one's seen,
It's a little bit of everything.

* * *

Earlier that day, Leslie had asked if I had heard anything yet from the doctor. I hadn't. "Next week, I figure," I had told her. I tried to forget about it. And as we left the theater and moved in baby steps across the parking lot and over the commuter train tracks in an unrelenting snowfall, my prostate was a buried thought. The weather had become icy, slippery, and hard to see, the airborne flakes fogging up the little bit of light emanating from the street lamps. But we had no control over the weather or the conditions, or anything else, and the night was unfolding as only the stars had planned. Navigating our way may have been tricky, but it didn't matter. We simply locked our arms together and stepped forward, never believing there might be a chance we could fall.

Chapter 13

I sat in a black high-back wooden chair at the round oak table I used as a desk and held the old Yamaha in my lap, adjusting strings, trying to keep the instrument tuned. The damaged tuner key—the one that gave me trouble before the contest in Virginia—had been acting up again. But like so many times before, I was working around it, making due. A truck rolled by on the street, rattling the front windows. I heard the voices of what sounded like two young women, talking as they walked presumably from the bar around the corner. It was midnight on the day after the Dawes concert, and I was alone at the apartment, but alone I wasn't.

I had most of the words now, I thought. Since working on the lyrics at Starbucks, I had made some minor changes, but hadn't played the chords or sang the melody in almost a month. I thought I had forgotten and I would have to mine my musical head to find the notes. Completing the song before Valentine's Day had been my goal, but that never happened.

I struggled to recall the structure—plucking at notes, strumming and then picking my way through chord progressions. It was there somewhere. And in time, piece-by-piece it came back to life. A note there and a chord change here. But even after the rediscovery, I wasn't completely satisfied. *Maybe I should build the song with picking first then strumming, playing full chords in the chorus.* I'd been at it for more than an hour and the tips of my fingers were stinging. I had played very little over the last few months and the callouses were nearly healed. I was tender and sore.

More people walked by outside, this time a man and woman. I could hear them arguing, snapping at one another in the bitter night air. A barking dog, seemingly responding to the couple's exchange, peppered the disagreement. I couldn't make out particular words, but was able to catch a few—*I can't believe it,* she said. *You're really being bitchy,* he said.

I played a D chord, picked the strings, and studied my computer screen where I had written the lyrics in a Word document. The screen glowed, but the only lamp on in the apartment was a small table light near the big leather chair, shining a soft light on the wall near the kitchen and on the painting of a tree. I could see parts of it in the shadows—gray and green and gold, a whimsical fairytale of a living thing. Leslie's daughter had painted it, an expression of the visions in her head. Behind me was a large photograph on canvas, the image of a black bicycle leaning against an ancient wall in France. Casey had captured this during a trip to Paris years ago. Across from the room on a bookshelf was a ceramic bowl, shaped by my son Graham, handmade with mud and embedded horsehair that ornamented the bowl with delicate black swirls in the beige clay. And to my right—obscured in the darker part of the room—a painting, oil on cardboard, a textured, bold rendering of flowers in a vase framed in barn wood, the work of a high school student who painted with her feet. I loved these things—expressions, statements of emotion and thought. They had given me comfort and still did. But now I was trying to create another kind of art— a song, the one before me, the one trying to fully materialize. *Why do I do this? Why do I write songs? No one's paying me. No one wants me to record and sell this music. Why did Leslie's daughter paint that tree? Why did Graham create that bowl in exactly that manner? Why did that bike speak to Casey? Why did the high school girl take off her shoes and dip her toes in oil paint?* At first blush, the answer is simple: to express ourselves. However, as I labored to rediscover the lost melody and fine-tune the lyrics, I found myself thinking less about the process of self-expression and more about the reason I was writing the song, the reason art was being created at all. I continued to grind through a methodical musical process of quarter notes and treble clefs in four-four time. But the heart of what I was attempting to build was not mechanical; the heart of it was a woman. She was its soul. The photograph, the ceramic bowl, the paintings around me offered their own gifts, but they are physical things; you can hold them. One would have to go to where they are to understand them, be in their physical presence to discover what they might mean or say to you. Prehistoric paintings are found on cave walls, but like the art objects in my home, one has to stand next to them to truly experience them. Music is a visceral, emotional dance like no other, unique but yet universal. Songs—including the ancient ones—forever float in the air. They are in us all, in our DNA. The very first melodies have been carried from primordial times and remain endless. We can call up a song—even make one up—in the shower, on a bus, on a car ride with the windows down. In my own small way, the song I offered to the crowd and the judges in Virginia was part of this primal wonder. And here I was again, trying to create another song, one of love that might resonate alongside the songs created thousands of years before.

Maybe I was just thinking too hard.

I heard more voices from outside along the front sidewalk. This time a young woman's gentle laugh is mixed with a man's confident cadence. These voices were sweeter than what I had heard before. Again, I couldn't make out specific words, but it was clear that he had something to say and she liked what it was.

I had rediscovered most of the melody now and began playing through the chorus, a pattern of simple G, F, and C chords. The lyrics started to slowly match the melody.

I wait for you to shine.
It's the sun in the heart,
The light from the dark.
From out of the dawn . . . you shine.

* * *

110

I sang the first verse and the second. I sang them again and again. I rewrote the third. I changed a minor riff in the chorus. I put the capo on the guitar's third fret and sang in a different key. And I began again. First verse. Second. Third. I took off the capo. I adjusted the chorus's melody, but only slightly. I sang it all the way through over and over.

The yelp of a police siren cut through the front windows into my apartment, the flashing blue light catching the edges of the tree painting. For an instant the tree appeared to move, as if it were animated. My dog barked at the window until the siren faded. Then, the night fell silent. I savored the quiet but within seconds I broke through it with the forceful strum of a D chord and a full singing voice. The song—for anyone who could hear it on the street or the apartments nearby—wasn't quite there yet. I wasn't yet content with it. But in the moment, it was becoming the best song I'd heard in a long time.

* * *

Leslie and I had a Sunday morning routine: KCBO in Denver streaming over the Internet, I read the *New York Times* online, and Leslie bounced between checking emails and considering whether to put oranges in the smoothies. In a few weeks, we'd be traveling to Seattle to see my son and first visit Portland to see The Decemberists kick off their tour. The tickets were a holiday gift for Leslie.

"I'm going to toss in just a couple of wedges. Gets too sweet," she said, knifing through an orange on a cutting board next to the mini blender on the counter near the kitchen sink. "The smoothies might be a little brown this morning. Happens when you put in blueberries with the kale. You okay with that?"

"Good to go," I said, my eyes fixed on a story on the *Times* website about Bill O'Reilly of Fox News and allegations he lied in his broadcast reports on the Falklands War years ago. *Mother*

Jones published a story a few weeks earlier that suggested he had embellished or fabricated facts. "What a scuzball this guy is," I murmured. I'm certain Leslie never heard me.

The blender whirred then stopped. She poured some liquid into a glass.

"How are you packing for Seattle?" Leslie asked, handing me the smoothie mix—not brown but beige in color and full of froth. "Try this. See if it's okay."

I took a sip.

"Not sweet enough for you, is it?" she asked.

"No, no it's fine. Good. Disgusting color," I smiled, "but I'll drink it."

"Yeah, not so appetizing." Leslie made great smoothies. Believed in them. Kale was always an ingredient. It was her go-to green. She has a photograph of herself at Kale Fest in Iowa, smiling proudly.

"Very light. I'm packing light," I said.

"Really?" Leslie grimaced. "I know we are doing the train to Seattle and all that, but I need things."

"No fancy dinners or anything. Think like we're going to a hostel in Europe." I suggested. I wanted us to be nimble travelers. We were staying four days in a small rented apartment near my son's place in Seattle's Ballard neighborhood, we'd have no car, and we'd take the Amtrak train from Portland to Seattle the morning after the Decemberists' concert. There was no reason for big suitcases.

"But I'm meeting your son," she said. "I want to wear nice boots and have a decent change of clothes."

Leslie can look good in a sheet, but she likes to be put together. She's not vain. She's aware. She knows what she likes and what works for her—simple, straightforward, but adorned with art—a collection of funky bracelets, a dangly necklace. She's a sophisticated hippie. She wears it well. But I had not considered until that very moment that this trip, as much as it was about a gift given to Leslie for Christmas and a celebration of what we loved together, it would also be her first encounter with my older son — the old soul, the photographer, the hiker, the artsy one, the thinker. The one who holds his cards close but feels deeply. Unlike Graham, Casey would be the one to consider more closely how Leslie was fitting into his father's life, and ultimately into his. While Graham would reach out his arms to accept, Casey would consider first what was before him. He would not judge, but he would observe with keen eyes, reaching out to embrace only what he believed to be authentic.

"I get that, sure," I said, taking another sip from the smoothie. "It'll be fine, you know?"

"I know we're trying to go easy, but I'm going to need one of those roller bags. That okay?"

Leslie asked that quite often. *That okay?* It was involuntary, as if she had been conditioned to request approval. I knew that wasn't the case; she wasn't asking me or anyone else for consent or permission. The question seemed to be a leftover reflex, a verbal tick from past relationships, an automatic request for acceptance from men who tried to shape her out of clay.

"You can take whatever you want."

"Well, it's going to be more than you," she laughed.

"This trip is not some test, you know? Casey is going to love you."

"I know I'm going to like him. He's like his dad."

"Well, a little, but he's his mother, too," I said. I pulled up a photo Casey had texted me the morning of the mountain trek. "This is where he went hiking this weekend. Lake Serene."

Mountains framed a photo of his dog, Cody. The message read *Good Morning.*

"Wow," Leslie said. "And I know I'm going to love Seattle."

"Why do I live here?" I asked. A rhetorical question I had tossed around a great deal during a bitter winter. "There are so many wonderful places. Places better than boring Illinois."

"Where would you want to go when you don't want to work anymore?" Leslie asked, taking a seat next to me at the breakfast counter, her smoothie in her hand.

"I'm always going to work a little. But I'd consider the Northwest. Maybe not Seattle. Too expensive."

"Oregon?" she asked. "Portland would be cool. But I heard Eugene is great and cheaper." Her laptop was on the counter. She turned and moved the mouse and opened a browser. "Let's just look at house prices for fun."

Suddenly, I was moving to Oregon. I was buying a house near the university. I was teaching part-time. I was hiking the nearby trails and making day trips to the Pacific Ocean. Leslie and I were decorating a small, quirky house not far from the college library, a cool place where we could watch the world pass from a perfectly placed, comfortable couch near the window. There would be a garden.

KCBO filled in the spaces with Simon and Garfunkel's "The Boxer", and when Leslie closed the laptop and reached across the counter to take my hand, it was as if she had decided something.

"By the way," Leslie asked. "Did you ever get those test results?"

I had not. Not yet. It had been more than a week.

* * *

Leslie's parents were making the transition from the home they had lived in for more than forty years to a one-floor condo—smaller, fresher, cleaner, more accessible, no yard—and Leslie had taken on the job of making it work. She had sold their house and found them a new place not far from the old home. It was perfect. Although her parents—her mother in her seventies, her father in his eighties—were initially reluctant, they finally saw how the move made sense. Leslie convinced them it was the right choice at the right time. They still could see their friends regularly, her father could continue working part-time at the flower shop, her mother could still visit the library and have lunch with her cronies. But decades of living in their split-level had invited chaos. Name it—it was stuffed in a cupboard, a storage closet, under the bed, or in the garage.

"Got something for you," Leslie said with delight, walking into my apartment before we would head out to a favorite Vietnamese restaurant down the street. She held a large-handled bag in her hand. "Wait 'til you see this."

It was an ornate ceramic container—a narrow, compact pitcher with a spout and a cork, about the size of a bottle of whiskey in the colors of Victorian blue, beige, white and yellow, and in the middle was the raised rendition of an ear of corn, symbolic of its contents—bourbon.

"Jim Beam!" Leslie announced. "Look at this. It has to maybe twenty-five years old? At least that's what my dad thinks."

"Must have been a gift," I said. "Wow. Probably made for the company's anniversary date or something."

"You think it's still any good?"

"Old bourbon? Probably."

The cork had eroded. There was a crack and evidence of moisture.

"You should keep this," said Leslie.

"Let's try it." *I* would try it, not Leslie. I carefully wedged the cork from the spout and took a simple, uncertain sip. "You know what? It's not bad."

"Really?"

"A bit strong, I think. Maybe not as smooth, but it's drinkable."

"You can throw it out if you want. I just thought—"

"No, no. Not throwing it out. It's cool." I really wasn't positive the liquor was any good. But I wasn't going to cast doubt. Not when Leslie thought of me, thought of how I loved good bourbon now and then, and had taken the time to cautiously wrap it up and lug it to my place.

"Would you make a Manhattan with it?" Leslie asked.

"I think you could do that," I said.

"My dad had it stuffed away with a bunch of other alcohol. Mom and Dad must have taken one sip out of it. Well, probably not my mother."

I removed a glass from the cupboard, cracked open an ice tray and dropped in four cubes.

"I'm going to have a bit more," I said.

Leslie smiled. "Seriously, you don't have to keep it."

I kissed her and poured two fingers worth of the vintage Jim Beam in the glass. The ice snapped as the golden liquor rolled over the cubes. I poured Leslie a small glass of red wine and toasted her father and mother; I toasted the gift giver of years ago; I toasted Leslie. And as Leslie sipped her wine, I tipped my glass and into my mouth I accepted the familiar bite of aged, slightly chilled bourbon.

"Nice," I said.

We savored a little silence.

"Haven't slept well the last couple days," I said, changing the subject.

"Oh," Leslie said. "What's that all about?"

"You're going to laugh," I said.

My dreams had always been like LSD trips—weird, colorful, out of sync, out of context, erotic, exotic, fantastical. Think "Lucy in the Sky With Diamonds."

"Flying pigs?" she asked, referring to a dream I had once told her about.

"No. I dreamed I had to pee and couldn't."

"Okay."

"I think it's the prostate thing."

"Or you were in that half-sleep time and you really did have to pee."

"Yeah, maybe."

"You're worried," she said.

"Maybe." I swirled the ice in the glass.

"Call them. They should have the test results by now. They probably just forgot. Someone misplaced them," she said. "It's nothing." Leslie knew a few things about waiting for test results.

"I'd prefer not to have that dream again," I said. "Flying pigs? Sure. That's better than a peeing nightmare."

"You should have some of those dreams analyzed," she said.

"Another thing," I said, pausing for a moment. "Would you ever go to back to Pittsburgh with me?"

"Another road trip?"

"I haven't been back since my mother died."

"And when was that?"

I reminded Leslie of my mental block, not remembering the date of my mother's death, or my father's. I quickly calculated that it had been somewhere around three years since Mom died, about six since Dad.

"I am a terrible person. What son doesn't remember these things?"

"Of course I would go back with you, if you think you need to."

I hadn't been to their graves since the funeral and it all felt unfinished. I took another sip of the old bourbon.

"Damn prostate," I said.

We finished our drinks and headed around the block for Vietnamese pho.

Chapter 14

The effort to complete the deal on Leslie's parents' condo was moving forward, but the house being sold was Leslie's childhood home and her clients were her parents, so this deal was far different from the usual real estate transaction. The hiccups and demands and negotiations had been heightened by familial history, tugs at the heart, and uncertainties. *Was this really the best thing for them? Are they going to be okay? Can they manage a move like this?*

"I just want them to be proud of what I can do for them, you know?" she asked. We were having dinner in a small Mexican restaurant in her neighborhood, eating fish and pork street tacos and taste testing several of the two dozen kinds of salsa offered at the salsa bar. We had a coupon.

"And they will be proud," I encouraged.

"This thing could still fall through," Leslie cautioned.

I drank from my bottle of Corona Light.

"The loan?" I asked.

"The buyer might have an issue. Single mom. Don't know what her complete situation is and, of course, my parents have to sell so they can buy."

"You're doing everything you possibly can," I said. It was a dumb thing to say, a clichéd response that meant little.

"Not sure I like this pork," Leslie said, after tasting one of her tacos.

"And that," I said, pointing to one of the salsas, "is smokin' hot. You'll probably love it."

I was a wimp when it came to spicy. Leslie could handle the heat.

This side of Leslie I had been seeing was new to me—working long hours into the late evenings, fretting over negotiations and details. In addition to the worry over her parents' well-being, she was hyperalert, hyperattentive to the pending deal. It was what she needed to do at the time. But I was selfish. *What about me?* We had been in lockstep through our lives so far together, but now she was building a new clientele and being pulled away. It was all for good reason, yes. Still, I was being a baby about it and embarrassed by what I sometimes felt.

"I meant to tell you that I am sorry," I said, tasting the beer again.

"For what?"

"I was in that funky place a while ago, sort of moody."

"Yeah, I felt bad."

"You know it has nothing to do with you, right?"

Leslie nodded, smiled. She had heard me ask that before. The sullenness began in fits and starts weeks before when I started trying again to write music, still confounded by my Valentine's Day song for Leslie. Yes, there had been progress but still no song. I was insecure. I was melancholy. It was the creative curse.

"You seem better," Leslie said. "Did you exercise?"

A big proponent of endorphins, Leslie was convinced I could physically work my way out of the funk. It worked for her. Yoga was behind most of it, she insisted. I knew that was part of it, but I was less convinced of the ultimate power of a workout, the warrior pose or a bike ride. It had taken me decades, but I knew I was hyperalert to emotions—my own and others. I swallowed them down—the poison or the medicine. It was just who I was. Still, I had taken her advice.

"Made a new bike playlist on Spotify," I said proudly.

"Yeah, but did you get on the bike?"

I had a stationary bike at my apartment. It was not quite springlike enough to regularly ride outside. She was joking, but it was a legitimate question.

I gave Leslie the *seriously?* look. "Yes, I've been on the bike." I pulled up the songs on my phone.

"I have to have serious rock 'n' roll. It has to jack me up. Get me going," I said. Then I rattled off the selections. "'Radioactive', Imagine Dragons; 'Gimme Stitches', Foo Fighters; 'Jealous Again', The Black Crowes; 'Renegades of Funk', Rage Against the Machine; 'Woodstock', Crosby, Stills, and Nash. That's from the Rock and Roll Hall of Fame concert. It's killer."

"Okay," Leslie acknowledged, dipping a chip in the hot salsa I was avoiding.

"'Won't Get Fooled Again'," I continued.

"Oh, love that."

"'Gotta Get Away', The Black Keys. 'Train in Vain', The Clash."

"*You* like The Clash? A bad eighties band?"

"I love The Clash."

"'Gimme Shelter', my favorite Stones song; and 'Sweet Jane',
from the band with the best name for a band in the history of the world—The Velvet Underground."

"I like the version from the Cowboy Junkies."

"Too druggie for me. Velvet."

"We even like the same kind of heavy music," Leslie said, as if she had just proven something to herself. "Seriously."

"And yes, we do, and yes, I've been on the bike, and yes, I feel better."

"Knew it."

"I'm still sorry. I wasn't exactly a gem to be around."

Leslie reached out and touched my arm. "Are you ready for Oregon?" she asked, taking a nibble out of her last taco.

I was certainly ready for Oregon and Portland and The Decemberists and all that good music; ready for Seattle, evergreen trees, mountains, great coffee and coffee shops, and Percy's & Company, my son's favorite bar in Ballard. I was more than ready for my son, whom Leslie would finally meet and I hadn't seen since his Christmas visit to Chicago. I was ready for the cool apartment Leslie and I had booked. And I was ready for a midnight view of the stars, ready for each tiny shimmering point of light that would peek out from behind the silvery clouds that bring the legendary rain to America's Pacific Northwest.

* * *

It had been a snowy, bitter February and early March and with just a few weeks from the start of spring, the weather was finally rewarding all of us for being patient. Warm temperatures were now giving Chicago a big hug. Although I had to dodge puddles of melted snow on my walk from the CTA train stop near my apartment, the sun and the chirp of birds helped me to forget about the little dance I had to perform around the pools of water and forget about the day at the college. There had been slashes in budgets and departmental changes. Lower enrollment had recently soured the work and the mood at the school. There were times it felt less like I was employed at a university and more like I worked a shift at a steel mill.

"Medium, four shots?" the barista asked. It was late afternoon. The coffee shop just down the street from the train stop and a block from my apartment was a frequent stop when I needed to decompress or a new venue in which to write. Like the character Norm—the barfly from the old TV show *Cheers*—I had become a regular at Counter Coffee.

"Bring it on," I said, and set my backpack down on a table near the window.

"Going for an afternoon pick-me-up?" The barista, a young guy who was usually there in the morning and sometimes in the late day, regularly wore a Blackhawks cap and a plaid shirt with the tails hanging out.

"Just missed the place," I answered.

Truth was, I was thinking about the song again. It was bugging me. I had the lyrics, I thought, but now I was reconsidering, believing they needed more effort, maybe even an overhaul. On the train, I had bounced around syllables and rhymes in my head and thought I might be discovering something new and fresh. But what was it? What was I discovering? I didn't know. And I still wasn't sure why this song had become such a long-term struggle and why I had not been completely pleased with what I was coming up with.

I opened up my bag and pulled out a small black Moleskine journal, clicked a pen and scanned my brain for the verses I had constructed during the train ride.

You said to me once
How did you ever find me
All those past lives
And all I've left behind me
You said to me once
Give me all you have left to give
All the past broken hearts
All that we forgive

* * *

Inside the coffee shop, I worked again with the syllables, the sounds, the verbal beats. I played with synonyms and different rhymes. After a half hour or so, I felt, maybe, I had something better than what I had written on the train. Hell, it wasn't Lennon and McCartney. Not Dylan or Leonard Cohen. But maybe it was finally coming to life. Maybe this version would be the one.

I whispered the words, over and over, trying to expose their natural rhythm.

"What was that?" the barista asked from behind the counter, after hearing my murmuring. I was puzzled how he noticed my soft singing over the whir of the espresso machine.

"Oh no, nothing," I said. Not the first time I had been discovered talking to myself.

I transcribed the verses a second time in the journal, printing them out with care as if savoring each word. When I was done, I looked out to the street. There, through the window to the sidewalk, I could see an older man walking his English bulldog, a young woman in tight black running pants and a purple Nike cap jogging across the street toward the shop, and a blind man with his white cane edging slowly toward the crosswalk. He paused near the light pole and waved his cane a couple of inches above the ground, finding his way. Of the three now waiting at the corner, only the blind man was smiling.

"Here you go," the barista said, setting a white ceramic coffee cup on a saucer in front of me.

"Nice work," I said.

"Best I could do today," he said. On top of the skim latte was the white foam of the milk's froth formed in the shape of a turtle, as if looking at it from above. "Symbol of adaptation," he said.

"It is?" I asked.

"Carries the energies of pace, patience, protection."

"Who knew?"

"Just doin' my thing," he said.

The crossing light had changed at the street corner. The man with the dog stepped from the curb and walked briskly across the four lanes of paused traffic, the woman accelerated, hitting her stride within seconds, but the blind man waited, waved his cane and tapped the concrete before him. Then with a particular kind of confidence, he strode across the street, indisputably certain of where he wanted to go.

I asked the barista if he knew whether the record store down the street was still open. He said he wasn't sure of the store's hours. I knocked back what remained of the coffee and headed there anyway. Although I may have been on a little roll with the song lyrics that late afternoon, and it might have been best to stay at the coffee shop to keep working, maybe the record store could somehow validate the work I had already done and finalize what had become such an arduous process.

Old School Records sits inside a fifty-year-old brick storefront, small and dusty, with hundreds and hundreds of albums in bins and on the floor along the walls. I had visited when I first moved to the neighborhood nearly two years ago, but not since. Many of the albums were tucked tightly into wooden racks. You had to stand to see the front covers, slipping each individual one out just far enough to take a closer look. The bands, the album art, the cover conditions were victims of time. A Boston album from the 1970s—the one with the spaceship on the front—had terribly tattered corners. But there were also others in better shape, including a Blue Oyster Cult record with songs I had never heard before, an obscure album that appeared nearly new. There was also an album from a band I had never heard of before—Niagara. On the cover, displayed in psychedelic font just below the band's name was a close-up photograph of a woman's sweaty left breast. The store clerk—a man in his forties wearing a black Metallica T-shirt—saw me reading the liner notes on the back cover.

"Rock fusion," he said. "Some Brazilian influences. The band members were German, though."

"They have a hit?"

"Maybe in Europe. But Billy Idol helped produce the record, I think."

I scanned the notes again to see if Idol's name was there. I couldn't find it.

"Anything you looking for?" the clerk asked.

"Not really. Just maybe a little inspiration."

I'm certain he didn't know what I meant and wasn't interested in investigating further.

"Let me know if I can help at all," he said, returning to the checkout counter in the center of the shop.

Vinyl records were supposed to be a dead music format—old and forgotten years ago. But just when it seemed no one cared anymore, someone did. Just as they were about to disappear into obscurity, they persevered. I can only speculate why, but it may lay in the physical experience, the interaction between you and the record. You clean the vinyl with a soft cloth, you delicately hold it by the outside edges so as not to smudge or scratch it, you gently balance it on the turntable's spindle, let it drop into place, and carefully allow the stylus to contact the outer groove. There is that familiar hiss, that crackle, and then guitar, drums, bass, and the human voice. It's a special relationship with vinyl—the album art, the liner notes on the cover—like the poems once written for a lover, the photographs of the sunny days you spent together, the love letters you saved. The tiny scratches and skips in the vinyl are frayed recollections of what once had been, and yet we hang on to the music and the memories, hoping to resurrect the best of the past to help us discover what is next.

I didn't truly understand why I had come to the store, why I was rummaging through the old records. *Inspiration? Honestly?* Years ago, I got rid of nearly all of my vinyl records—dozens of them. *Abbey Road* and the first Led Zeppelin album were among them. And even though I no longer owned a record player and didn't plan to buy one, I regretted letting those records get away. Still, I was not there to right that wrong. I was there for something else. Maybe there was a spark of lyrical brilliance in the store somewhere that could give me nourishment. Or maybe, with all the music in front of me—much of it decades old—I would better understand the passage of time and that might fuel my songwriting. Certainly some of the records contained the music that once burst from the speakers of the record player in my teenage bedroom and some of it was the music I performed years ago in the band and as a solo performer. Maybe there was some motivation in that. Or maybe the vinyl albums were casting long shadows directly on the songs I had written as a young man—the music I wrote in my college days, even the song I carried with me to Virginia and the song I was now trying to finish. Maybe I was there simply to remind myself what songwriting was really about for me. It was not about making records, being a rock star. It was about opening up, letting others into my heart like handing them a page from a diary. Since my first pluck of a guitar string, that had been my constant—playing songs that said what I felt. So many things have changed, but even now in the October of my life, I know this remains. I am not the person I was at eighteen, twenty-five, thirty-five, or forty-five. I'm only tiny pieces of my former self. It's what happens to all of us. We are never who we think we will become, and searching is all for show. There is a Buddhist teaching that suggests our search to "find ourselves" is useless. There is no hidden *us* below all of life's layers. We are forever changing, evolving. It's foolish to lock in our futures, to plan for what we think we want to be at any age. We will only be disappointed. But maybe the core of each of us is always there, always centered no matter what. The vinyl records in the stacks at Old School Records hold the songs of musicians who, in their time, believed they were creating meaningful art, expressions that would last forever. But now, thousands of notes on the hundreds of albums are irrelevant to fresh ears, their impact lost in the years. However, we all know there are some songs, like ancient melodies, that have remained significant to those who will listen. Somewhere inside all of the stacks of records at Old School is a buried gem pressed in black vinyl, waiting to be found, a song the passage of time could not diminish, the one constant in all the changes. I did not uncover that hidden jewel that evening, but the belief that it was there somewhere might have been the inspiration I needed.

"Thanks," I said, stepping toward the record store's door. "You have a great place here."

The clerk smiled and waved an acknowledgement as I exited empty handed. As I stepped to the sidewalk in front of the store, I heard the door of the store lock behind me. A man and woman holding hands and laughing walked by and stepped into the Italian restaurant next door. A couple of teenage boys zipped past on skateboards. I turned west and took the crosswalk to the north side of Madison Street, walked near the Hallmark card shop, the antique store, and Shanahan's bar and headed the long way home.

Chapter 15

I snapped a phone photo of the front cover of *Turtle Island* and sent it with a text to Leslie.

Standing in line to get Snyder to sign it, I wrote.

Writer boner, she replied.

I laughed loud enough for the woman standing in front of me to turn around. "Funny text," I said. She smiled.

The phrase *writer boner* came from Graham. My son frequently poked fun at what he thought was my geeky passion for writers and songwriters. Leslie heard him joking with me once and remembered the exchange.

Gary Snyder had come to Columbia as part of a festival hosted by the Creative Writing Department. A week of *writer boners*, you might say. I wouldn't say I was a huge fan of Snyder, although I had some of his poetry on my shelves. His work had won many prizes, including the Pulitzer, but the biggest draw for me was his connection to Jack Kerouac. Snyder was Japhy Rider, the Zen master and spiritual center of Kerouac's *The Dharma Bums*. Although he had grown to be an old man, it was the young Snyder that fascinated me. That night at the college event, it was clear the heart of Japhy was still beating.

"Old men still have new ideas," Snyder said. The poetry professors, wearing black sweaters and sporting white beards nodded, and students wrote those words from Snyder in their Moleskines, as if they were compelled to record every utterance. "What do you aspire to be in the world? And how can we harness our talents with the most impact?" he asked, challenging the artists before him. This eighty-year-old man, wearing a white shirt, black vest, and Buddha beads around his neck stood at the podium with a straight back and a wide smile. He still had his hair, his bushy beard, and his voice was strong enough not to need the microphone at the podium. He reminded me of Bob

Dylan, whom Leslie and I had seen perform recently at the Chicago Theater.

Snyder confidently read from his new book of poems. He was not arrogant nor did he offer his words as some poetic sermon. Snyder was simply sharing with palpable grace. I leaned toward the English professor I knew sitting a chair away and whispered, "Have you seen him before?" He shook his head and smiled, "But I'm glad I didn't miss this."

"This poem is from the time I spent with the forestry workers in the Northwest as a young man," Snyder told the crowd. I believe he said he was eighteen or nineteen at the time, and had been baling hay for one reason or another, working ten- to twelve-hour days. "There was this old man with us and he was keeping up with the young guys. I remember him saying, 'When I was a young man, I told myself I wouldn't want to be doing this all my life. Well, damn it, that's just what I've gone and done.'"

The crowd laughed but Snyder did not. Clearly, this wasn't meant to simply be an amusing story.

He read the poem with reverence slowly and softly. It was only a few lines but said a book's worth. He read another about a hike with a friend, another that was a response to a letter from an aspiring poet, he talked about the wildfires in California, how sometimes fires are essential and destruction is a good thing, and how he lives on the fifty-thousand-year calendar, starting with the date of the first known work of art. An hour after he began, he closed his books and sighed. "I will leave you with this," he said. "For those of you who are creating art, writing and teaching, consider what the Buddhists say: 'Hold it close, then give it away.'"

I had finally made my way to the front of the table where Snyder had been sitting, signing books and speaking briefly with admirers.

"It is a pleasure, Mr. Snyder," I said. I shook his hand and gave him my new copy of *Turtle Island*. He looked frailer up close, his face and hands spotted by age, his fingernails long, dark, and hardened. "What's the circa on the photo?" I asked.

"The what?" He appeared slightly confused.

"The photo." I pointed to the picture on the back cover.

"Oh, yes." He thought for a moment. "It's 1974 maybe?"

"I presume this is your son?" It was a candid photo. The young Snyder—long hair pulled back in a ponytail—smiled as a young boy, just barely noticeable behind him, peeked over his shoulder.

"Yes," he said, focusing for a few seconds on the photo, his fingertips softly touching the picture. Without looking up, he asked, "Sign it on the first page?" He did not wait for an answer. Just below the book's title page, he wrote his name in black ink.

* * *

I walked out to the sidewalk along Michigan Avenue where dozens of students had gathered to smoke. The chilly air kept the white puffs lingering in the air longer than you might think. I sat on one of the big concrete planters along the walkway, opened *Turtle Island*, and looked at Snyder's handwriting. *I wished he had written more*, I thought. *Something personal. Maybe my name? I could have asked, I guess.*

I called Leslie on the walk to my car.

"So how was Japhy?" she asked. Leslie was supposed to come with me to the Snyder reading but had a wake to attend; the father of her daughter's friend had suffered a massive stroke.

"Japhy was great. More than I expected," I said. Truthfully, I didn't know exactly what I expected.

"Anyone ask about *The Dharma Bums*?"

"I think he's tired of talking about that. But no, no one asked." I secretly wished someone would have. "How was the wake? If that's how you're supposed to ask about that sort of thing?"

"It was okay. They're doing all right. Next few days will be the toughest. You know how that is."

"You'd have liked this thing, babe. Snyder really was engaging." I wanted to talk more about the night, about the swirl of feelings that had arisen while listening to Snyder read and talk. I wanted to talk about old age and art, about having something to say, about Zen simplicity and nature, about what the future might bring, about us, but nothing was truly clear somehow. There were only undefined scattered emotions and sensations. We were a couple of days away from our trip to the Northwest, The Decemberists' concert, and visiting my son, and I believed I needed—right then and there—affirmation of my closeness to Leslie, to be guaranteed the synapses between us were vigorously snapping. This was not unfamiliar territory, this need to connect. It had been there before—the feelings had been there after the songwriting competition in Virginia and now after this night of poetry.

"I really liked what he had to say," I said.

"Writer boner?" she asked.

I laughed. "Yep. Writer boner."

"See you soon," Leslie said, before hanging up.

It wasn't until I returned to my car and sat inside that I noticed the notification of a voicemail on my phone. My doctor's office had left a message.

This is for David. We have your results but can't leave them in a message here. Please call when you can.

I telephoned first thing in the morning, talked to a nurse, and then called Leslie.

"Everything is fine," I said. "Everything is going to be okay."

"Didn't need to worry," she said.

I would have to get tests every year for the rest of my life. But for now, on this front, I was *not* taking after my father.

* * *

The plan was to take the El early Saturday morning to the radio station for my usual air shift and afterward hail a cab to the airport to meet Leslie.

"You'll die," Leslie insisted.

"I'm not going to die. I've been on the El a thousand times at weird hours."

"But this is three in the morning."

"It's okay."

It was a bit unnerving to think of taking the El through Chicago's Westside in the middle of the night, but I refused to let Leslie know about my marginal concerns.

"I really don't want to get a call from the morgue," Leslie said, exaggerating for emphasis.

I skipped the El and took a cab.

"What gets a nice guy like you out here in the middle of the night driving a taxi?" I asked the driver—a tall, lanky, polite man from West Africa—after he had picked me up on the street in front of my house.

"I'm a farmer. But it's off-season now and I bring my family here in the colder months to drive a cab."

His name was Maleek. He was soft-spoken, but quick to speak about what he loved. I could see his eyes glancing through the rearview mirror at me in the backseat.

"Mostly African vegetables. Peppers, for one. Organic. I distribute everywhere. I'm trying to buy more land. Ten acres now. I want ten more. Hoping to get a bank loan. Just waiting for the word."

"Maybe I've eaten some of your vegetables," I said.

"I hope you have," he said, smiling. "And you, sir? What do you do? Why are you coming into the city now? Most are leaving downtown and most are drunk?" Maleek laughed.

"Guess I'm breaking the rules a little, huh?"

I told him about my upcoming trip to the Northwest and the radio work.

"I listen to that station," Maleek said, turning up the volume on his dash radio. "So, I would hear you?"

"Yes, in a couple hours."

"That is very good, sir. I'm in the presence of a celebrity. That's pretty wonderful."

It was not unusual, this celebrity thing. I never have considered myself a celebrity of any kind, even with all the years of doing on-air radio work. But so many times when I tell people that I work on the radio, they are impressed or captivated.

"I just talk on the radio," I said.

Maleek pulled the cab to the east side of the Prudential Plaza not far from Lake Michigan where the station's studios were located. He stepped out to help me with my bag.

"There you are, sir," Maleek said. He shook my hand. "I'll be listening."

"Good luck with your vegetables and your loan," I said.

"I pray for good things, sir. Good things."

* * *

Somehow I missed meeting Leslie. I had texted her when I was about to go through security, suggesting to meet up at the airport gate, but when I got past the metal detectors and looked around, I couldn't find her.

Where are you? TSA get you? she texted.

I called her.

"I'm at the gate. Just got here," I said.

"I'm at security. How did you not see me?"

Never saw her. I figured she headed for the gate so I headed there. It's a small space outside the detectors, so it seemed curious that neither of us noticed the other.

We had that mishap at Red Rocks—losing the car, the keys, Leslie's reaction to the dope—I didn't want to start this trip on a rocky note. In the big realm of things, this was certainly not a big deal, but I had hoped everything would go super smoothly.

I walked back toward security and met Leslie halfway to help carry her luggage. "I thought you may have forgotten about something in your bag from the Colorado trip," Leslie said. "Some remnants sniffed out by a security dog or something."

"Oh, wow. No. That would not have been good," I said, tossing the strap of her bag over my shoulder.

"I had visions of you in some interrogation room."

"*Midnight Express,*" I joked.

The flight to Portland was scheduled to be more than three hours. We brought books. I had my notebook and my computer, thinking I might write.

"I never really asked you how the wake the other day weighed on you, did I?" I asked. We had settled quickly into our seats and the plane was already ascending, departing on time.

"Death is just weird no matter how you face it, see it, deal with it," Leslie said.

The man—the father of her daughter's friend—had died young. Mid-fifties. Apparently men in that family had a history of dying young. "How old was your father when he died?"

"Seventy-five?" I estimated. Again, like everything else about his death, I was uncertain.

"You got lots of time," Leslie said.

"I had my heart attack the same year as my dad," I said. "Different reasons but the same exact age. Strange."

"I'll die before you," she said.

"Come on."

"No, really. The cancer."

"But you're better now. And remember what killed my dad."

Leslie smiled, closed her eyes, and placed her head on my shoulder. I watched the clouds through the plane's window until both of us fell asleep. We were somewhere over the Rocky Mountains.

Chapter 16

"There are a lot of beards here," Leslie said.

We had arrived in Portland.

"Any other time I'd say that was stereotyping, but ..." I looked around inside the airport terminal—to the front, left, right, and behind. "You are absolutely right."

It was the hipster ensemble: bushy beard, flannel shirt, boots, maybe a piercing, and you could throw in a tattoo.

I carried both of our bags to the outside curb and we waited for Leslie's old college friend, someone she hadn't seen in years.

"You remember what she looks like?" I asked.

"I'll know her immediately. She doesn't change," Leslie said. "But I don't know the car or what Nick looks like."

Nick was Suzy's new boyfriend. They'd be arriving together. The plan was for to them drop us off at the hotel, we'd dump our bags, go to dinner with them, and then they'd take us to Keller Auditorium.

"There she is!" Leslie said, waving her hand high above her head.

Suzy was driving. She pulled her SUV to the curb and jumped out of the driver's seat.

"Oh, my god!" she said, wrapping her arms around Leslie.

"Nick?" I asked, reaching out my hand as we stood before the vehicle's open hatchback. "Nice to meet you."

"David, yes, so how do you like Portland so far?" he asked, helping me place the bags in the payload area.

"Warmer than Chicago, thank you very much."

"And plenty of beards," Leslie laughed, still standing near the curb with one of her arms entwined in Suzy's.

We took our places in the vehicle—Suzy back at the wheel, Nick in the front passenger seat, Leslie behind Suzy, me behind Nick.

"How long has it been?" I asked.

"Oh my, twenty years?" Leslie said.

"Yeah, I think so," said Suzy.

"Seems like weeks, right?" I asked.

"College does that," Nick said. "When we pulled up to the airport, I asked what does Leslie look like, do you remember?"

"She's hot," Suzy laughed. "You'll notice her."

I smiled. Leslie blushed.

"It's a long time ago," Leslie said, dismissing the compliment.

We had reservations at an old Portland standby—Jake's. But finding a place to park was a bit of a chore, so we kept driving around the downtown's grid.

"You know Powell's, right?" Suzy asked. The legendary bookstore was known all over America. "Thought I'd drive by and let you see the place."

We didn't have time to stop. The schedule was a little tight. Plus, going into Powell's would end up as an hours-on-end adventure. You don't go into Powell's for a moment; you go into Powell's for the day.

"It's the size of Macy's," I said, looking over Suzy's shoulder through the windshield. "Enormous."

"I love this downtown," Leslie said. "Just what I thought." The city had the feel of a well-read, dog-eared novel.

"Good place. Just don't call it a little Seattle," said Nick.

Portlanders bristled at that comparison.

Jake's was old school. Mahogany lined walls. Wooden booths. Waiters in white. Fish filled the menu. I ordered a Manhattan, Leslie a wine, Nick a beer. Suzy chose a Brazilian drink. The Brazilian mojito. Calamari and salmon would be ordered.

"Okay. Time to tell all. How'd you guys meet?" Leslie asked, sipping her cabernet.

The story involved eHarmony. They had been seeing each other for a couple of months. Leslie and I met on Match, so there was plenty to talk about—all those odd and awkward emails from dating frogs, the first dates that turned out to be achingly uncomfortable, and then finally finding someone.

"David doesn't have those stories," Leslie joked. "He seems to get along with everyone, even all his exes." She bumped my shoulder and smiled.

I had heard this so many times before. I can't remember a relationship that ended ugly, I mean *really* ugly. I was friends with my ex-wife, old girlfriends occasionally reconnected. I agreed it was different and at times created some tension between Leslie and me—especially when women from my past showed up on my Facebook page or out of nowhere sent me a text. It's not as if I was some sort of Casanova. Far from it. I just didn't throw people away. Sometimes I thought I should have.

"The girls met at college, right? Sorority?" I asked.

"Those were the days of dancing on the tables at some fraternity party," Leslie laughed.

"You danced on tables?" I asked.

"It was college," Leslie smiled. "There were times."

All of us had *times*.

* * *

The entrance to Keller Auditorium was abuzz. Scalpers hawking single tickets, a line a block long at the will call booth, fans taking one last drag on cigarettes before heading inside. We said goodbye to Suzy and Nick at the curb. There were hugs and handshakes.

Keller is ornate, grand in many ways, old but elegant. It was almost torn down years ago, but the people of Portland rose up and saved it with donations and petitions and civic meetings. There were renovations. The concert hall was reborn.

The opening act was forgettable. Not bad, just not something to write home about. But the folky band did give a preview into the kind of acoustics Keller would permit—rich and resounding.

When the lights went down for The Decemberists, there was loud and grand fanfare—an epic, tongue-in-cheek orchestral opening to introduce Colin Meloy, the band's lead singer and principal songwriter. With a mix of bearded hipster and childlike innocence, Meloy strode to center stage, wearing his signature sport coat, his acoustic guitar strapped around his shoulder and began to strum the simple opening chords to "The Singer Addresses His Audience"—a biting criticism of the music business, the popular song, commercialism, and celebrity. The crowd erupted and the cheers and applause built as the song grew in intensity.

"We're the Decemberists," Meloy told the crowd. "We're from here."

Although Meloy was born in Helena, Montana, he went to school for a time in Eugene and eventually moved to Portland for the music scene. It's home now. I would guess there was still a lot of Montana in Meloy. Not unlike all the Pittsburgh that is still in me despite the move to Chicago decades ago.

I grabbed Leslie's hand and held tight, watching her eyes as she watched Meloy. This was our moment, our time. This was Leslie's gift and mine, too. More than a vacation concert or the highlight of a trip to the Northwest, this night was our celebration day, our commitment day.

Meloy frequently switched guitars—acoustic to hollow-body electric—moving from song to song—ballad to folk rock. Young girls with flowers in their hair swayed to the sounds. Couples danced in the aisles.

"This is perfect," Leslie whispered, resting her head on my shoulder.

Meloy, an electric six string across his chest, slashed at the minor chord that opens "Make You Better." My stomach fluttered. Like Dylan's "Girl from the North Country," "Make You Better" would shake me up and I knew it. There would be a trembling lip, tears to hold back. All this would come hard; it would be unavoidable. I would try to hide it from everyone around me and from Leslie, but it would not be easy.

I don't pretend to know exactly what the song is trying to say. But there is a level of regret in those lyrics, a false belief that if we try hard enough and believe hard enough, we can make each other better, that the love of another can rescue us.

I could sense the water in my eyes and its escape from the outside corners, tears melting on my cheek. I turned to the wall just left of me and wiped the moisture away. I wasn't sure I understood the tears, but as the song gathered force, I sang its chorus under my breath as if I had no other choice. *Did past loves make me better? Did I make them better? Could Leslie make me better? Could I make her better? Were we about to save each other?*

When the chorus was repeated for the last time, the melody rose in the final words of the lyric, like a lover's last gasp, like a man holding his chest and his breath as he tries one last time to offer his heart to the one he loves. Then at the very end, the song returns to the minor chords of its beginning and finishes like an unanswered question.

I leaned into Leslie. "I absolutely love that song," I choked.

Leslie may not have noticed my heart on my sleeve, but she knew it was there.

The concert ended in a flurry of theatrics, and the eccentric Decemberists' song about whales and the sea. It was literary, lyrical, and kitschy at the same time. I usually dislike the mixture of music and theater in a rock performance, but this was light-hearted, playful. It made me smile. Standing to applaud, I wrapped my arm around Leslie's waist and pulled her tight to my side.

"That may have been one of the best concerts I've ever been to," I said, trying not to overdo it. The flush of a good concert has been known to overly influence your initial review. I saw James Taylor at the Civic Arena in Pittsburgh when I was nineteen and I thought I would never experience another night like it. That was until I saw Bob Dylan play in the gymnasium of Benedictine University, a small college outside Chicago. Then *that* was the night of all nights.

"Honestly, that was incredible," Leslie said, seemingly allowing the final notes of the show to linger in her head. "I'm a bit speechless."

The air outside the auditorium was cool and clean. It would be a pleasant walk to the hotel, but which way to go? I pulled out my phone and opened Maps. This was not going to be a repeat of Red Rocks. Leslie laughed as I punched the hotel address into the app.

"At least we're not high," she said.

"This way." I nodded toward the streetlight at the corner.

The rush of the hometown crowd had quickly dissipated. In just a city block, the energy of all those concertgoers had faded and now it was strangely quiet. Not in a mysterious way, but as if some higher power had cleared away a path for us. We were alone, holding hands, silent in our singular place in the world, slightly stunned, the way one is after the final scene of a great movie. It was as if we were the only people on Earth. Nothing and no one else mattered. I twisted my arm in Leslie's, trying to remain as close to her as possible as the city's nighttime sparkle opened up to us.

I am in love again. I am in love with the music, the Portland night, and with the woman on my arm. I was married for twelve years and I was in love then, and I was in love before that marriage and again after it, sometimes for months, sometimes for years. Sometimes I was good at it, sometimes not. Sometimes I may have been simply and unknowingly in love with love. But in every case, love sharpened my senses—I saw better, heard better, my heart beat stronger. I danced to love's melody; I heard its chorus. And here I am now on a deserted street in a celebrated city of the Northwest in love one more time.

We stopped at a corner to allow a car to pass and I touched

Leslie's hair, and rested my thumb on her cheek so I might softly stroke it. I was no longer a middle-age man with an old prostate and stent in my heart; I was young and tireless and full of promise. I was ageless. I was brand-new. And once inside the hotel room, I turned on only the bathroom lamp, allowing soft shadows to form on the walls and the light to glint off the small mirror above the low dresser. With Leslie facing away from me on the white sheets, I kissed her undressed back before sleep finally caught up to us.

Chapter 17

The Amtrak train was just minutes out of Portland when it turned north and rolled over a wide bridge.

"Is this the Columbia River?" I asked.

"I'm not sure," Leslie said, sleepily. We had taken a cab at 6:30 in the morning to arrive at Portland's Union Station in time for the #500 Cascades to Seattle. Being certain about whether or not you were traveling over the Columbia River wasn't so important when the body craves rest.

"It's the Willamette," I said, consulting the map I had pulled up on my phone.

"Ah," Leslie acknowledged.

"Columbia is next."

"And there's Vancouver," Leslie said, noticing through the train car's window a large sign announcing the city. "Is that what they were talking about last night?" She was puzzled. "I thought they were saying something about British Columbia."

At one point between songs, Colin Meloy teased the band's fans from Vancouver, Washington. Leslie and I didn't get the joke, assuming we had to be from Portland for it to translate.

"I guess that's like New Yorkers ripping on anyone from New Jersey. Chicagoans making fun of Hoosiers," I said. "Everyone has hometown pride, that *we're better than you* kind of thing."

We had quickly found comfort in the train's high-back seats, and our window was on the good side of the train, facing west. We had asked for the seats. Better views, we were told.

"Look at those homes. Like little boxes," Leslie said.

The houses sat tight along a small river or canal, some appeared to be resting on stilts or floating in the water. I wondered how they kept from falling over. And when the land opened up as we entered Washington State, the countryside began to tumble and roll. Pastures appeared; there were farms and ranches of intense green. As the train flashed past it all, I read the entertainment section of the *New York Times*. Leslie finished a few more pages of *The Dharma Bums*. And we napped, resting against each other, shoulder to shoulder. In four hours, we were in Seattle.

"He has an orange Element," I said, standing with Leslie next to our bags under the outside canopy at King Street Station, protecting ourselves from the drizzle. Casey had texted: 5 *minutes out.* There was one way into the passenger pick-up zone so it would be easy to spot him. "He'll have his dog, too. Guaranteed."

"You said he'll probably have a bunch of his camera equipment in the car," Leslie reminded me.

"Good thing we packed light," I laughed.

It had been a year since Casey moved to Seattle, and now anyone would have a hard time convincing him to leave. There was good hiking, better weather than Seattleites would ever let on, and more remarkable scenery than one lens could capture.

"Is that him?" Leslie spotted the big lunchbox of a vehicle pulling up near the far curve in the street. "Orange, right?"

"Hey," I hollered from where we stood at the station doors. Casey couldn't hear me. The car windows were rolled up. He stepped from the driver's side, his beard bushier than I remembered.

"There he is!" Cody was at the passenger side window, his doggy nose smudging the glass and his copper-colored ears at attention. Cody was a mix—Australian shepherd and something else, mostly likely Labrador—and weighed about fifty pounds. He was a rescue dog.

"Nice timing," Leslie said to Casey. "We got here just a few minutes ago."

I hugged Casey's tall frame, feeling shorter than the last time I had embraced him.

"Hey, man," I said, slapping his back. "This is Leslie."

"So nice to meet you," he said, extending a hand.

"Me, too. I feel like I already know you."

We stuffed our bags in the payload area and Casey let Cody out on the leash for a pee. The modern football stadium loomed just a couple of blocks away; its shadow would have dwarfed us if it had been sunny, and the brick rail station with the clock tower stretched into the gray sky like the steeple of a church in the center of an eighteenth-century Nordic village.

"Have I ever been in this part of town?" I asked, climbing into the rear passenger-side seat.

"I don't remember, Dad," Casey answered, playfully mocking me, as if that question was so very important.

"Well, *I* haven't," Leslie said.

Casey pulled his car out of the station's turnaround. We talked about our effortless train ride, Seattle's reputation for rainy weather, salmon, the abundance of coffee shops in Casey's neighborhood, walking Cody to his favorite grassy area behind the condo, and what Casey had in mind for a place to eat.

"Going to West Seattle. This little taco place right by the water," Casey said. "Would be better if it weren't raining."

"Just drizzle. No biggie," I said.

"I could go for a good taco," said Leslie. "Bring it on."

Marination Ma Kai is an earthy place inside a gray-and-white boathouse-style wooden building across from a stretch of the Puget Sound in downtown Seattle. There was a line out the door and a handful of regulars sat on the patio under big umbrellas, thumbing their noses at the misty weather. A few bicycles leaned against a horizontal metal pole on the strip of grass near the road. We ordered fish tacos and kimchi quesadillas, coleslaw, and bottles of beer. Cody slept in the car.

"You look good, bud," I said.

"Things are good," Casey said.

"Seattle suits you?" Leslie asked, knowing the answer.

Casey's smile answered her question.

We talked about Seattle's rainy days, the nearby mountains,

Casey's hiking travels in the Cascades, and his recent trip to Moab, Utah.

"I love your photos, Casey," Leslie said. I had shared some of Casey's nature photography on his website and Leslie had seen all the photos I had mounted in my apartment, including the electrical bicycle photo from France—the black, muddy bike leaning against the brick wall in a small village.

"Thank you," he said. "Been taking photos since I was a kid."

"One of those cameras you buy at the drugstore, first one, right?" I asked.

"Yeah, I think so," Casey laughed.

We talked about Casey's neighborhood, Ballard, and his work as a video editor. We talked about restaurants and the great seafood you could get. And we talked about his dad's dating. I honestly don't know how we got on that subject, but we did. I think Leslie joked about it somehow and that kicked it off. But there it was again, how Dad had dated *so many* women (it was only a few) and that they were all still *friends*, whatever that meant.

"They were amicable breakups, I said. "None of it was ugly."

"You're such a nice guy," Leslie smirked.

Casey offered a wry smile.

"I could be a jerk, you know," I said.

"Not in your nature," Leslie said. "Plus, I wouldn't be here if you were a jerk."

"Apparently you don't know him well enough," Casey added, grinning.

"Oh, nice," I said, playfully slapping Casey's arm.

"Ever have just *one* bad breakup?" Casey asked.

"Not really. Well, there was one that wasn't exactly perfect," I said. "It wasn't a mutual thing. I did the breaking up."

"One? That's it?" Casey asked.

"Not even with your mother," I said.

"Yeah, I'm aware," Leslie snickered. She was still getting used to the friendship I had with Casey's mother. It was a bit unusual, I'll admit. But we committed to be friends when we split and Casey and his brother were young, and we were still committed.

"I don't know how to be any other way," I added, and took a swig of beer.

The tacos went down quickly. Casey and I each had a second beer. And as the line at the door lengthened and the noise level inched up, Leslie headed for the restroom and Casey and I exited into the misty rain.

"Too bad it's so foggy. The view from here is very cool," Casey said, walking toward the car.

"It's pretty good as it is," I said, standing motionless in the drizzle so I could take all of it in.

"Is she okay?" Casey asked.

"Leslie? Yeah, why?"

"The talk about the old girlfriends."

"Oh, no. We've talked a lot about that. She's cool."

"She seemed a little upset."

"We joke about it," I said. "But it's still something to get used to. Her past relationships did not end well." I put my arm on his shoulder. "Are *you* okay?"

"Yeah, yeah. I guess maybe she is just hard to read."

"You just met her," I said.

What was in the boxes of my past lives wasn't an easy matter for Leslie and me. If the boxes would have been shut tight with duct tape, that's one thing. But much of my past lives often spill out of their containers. Still, we were being open and talking about it whenever it was necessary. But I knew it wasn't that simple. And maybe I didn't completely understand it myself. When a relationship ends, aren't you supposed to just tear it apart, throw it out? And sometimes I wondered: were these relationships really over for me? I was certain they were, in the romantic sense, but still, I have always had a hard time throwing people away.

145

Casey's condo was in a hundred-year-old coastal-style building next to a small church in a part of Seattle's historic seafaring neighborhood, founded by Swedes and Norwegians. We climbed the stairways, took off our shoes, and settled in. Casey poured two fingers of Tullamore Dew into a pair of tumblers, an Irish whiskey I had recommended to him years ago, even bought him a bottle once. This may have been the same bottle. It was nearly half-empty.

"Cheers," he said. "Welcome."

We clinked glasses.

"Sure you don't want one?" I asked.

"Whiskey is not my drink," Leslie said.

Casey and I sat on the leather couch in his apartment, Leslie in the chair opposite us, tugging on the doggy rope that Cody held tightly in his teeth. When Cody won the game, the dog settled in to chew.

"I have a little something for you," Leslie said. She handed Casey a gift bag. "My parents are moving and when I was helping to clean out all their stuff, I found this,"

It was a camera, black and silver, maybe from the 1930s or 1940s, German-made, a name I had not heard before.

"Oh, wow. Very cool," Casey said, studying the camera's details. On a high shelf in a small enclave off Casey's bedroom were a number of antique cameras. "This will fit right in." Casey stood, and motioned for Leslie to follow him. He placed the new addition next to a Polaroid Instamatic. "I'm going to have to do some research on that," he said. "Thank you. Thank you, very much."

I wanted to tell Casey then and there that in a few months Leslie and I would be moving in together, but thought twice about it, deciding it might be best to wait until father and son were alone.

* * *

Leslie and I had booked an apartment around the block from Casey's, a hundred-year-old cottage turned into an artist's studio. Narrow stairs led to thick wood plank floors. It was airy and coastal, like Casey's, but with fewer modern updates. The white porcelain kitchen sink was tucked in a small mudroom and although the plumbing worked fine, the bathroom still felt as if you had stepped into the 1920s. On the walls hung works of art—drawings, simple wire sculptures—the art of a woman with a pageboy haircut and a quick smile. Patti Shaw greeted us at the door near the small living room where she performed her daily work. Just inside the room were three large baskets of thousands of tiny aluminum wick holders from the burned candles at St. James church, candles that had once been lit to remember the dead. "Recycled prayers, I call them," she said. "Everyone needs prayers." Patti and the church had an arrangement. Near the window in the studio area was a dress, shimmery and silver, made from hundreds of those wick holders. In the upstairs bedroom, more art. Another wire sculpture of a plump Victorian woman hung near the door and on the wall behind the bed were dozens of singular faces, each one drawn in what appeared to be charcoal pencil on recycled paper about the size of a page from a paperback novel. "They're real people. People I've met, seen, noticed," Patti said. The faces were haunting and beautiful at the same time. *The art of real people,* I thought. *Isn't that what art is really about?* Portraits are not about the canvas or the colors or the medium, they're about the people. Literature is not about the words; it's ultimately about the people in those stories. And music, it too is about people, the songs written about them and for them. Patti knew this. She knew it better than I.

"Did you see the succulents in the sidewalk on the way up to the door?" Leslie asked, as we moved our bags up the twisting, tight stairway to settle in. "In the cracks?"

"In the concrete, around the stones?" I asked.

"The climate, the rain, it just brings out these beautiful living things," she said. "It's so lush."

Leslie noticed these things, a skilled observer, like an artist. Nature, plants, flowers are about people, too, aren't they? She recognized the splendor, authentically taking it in and letting it push against the heart, her eyes working right alongside her deepest humanity. This is what I wanted Casey to understand about Leslie, to know as I did. And it was certainly the under-lining reason I was in Seattle.

* * *

That night dinner was in Ballard at a small Italian restaurant with big windows that looked out onto a square in the shopping district made up of old redbrick buildings. A light rain fell, but streams of sun peeked through silvery clouds from time to time. We ordered pasta with vodka sauce, grilled salmon and baked white fish, and a bottle of red wine. We didn't care about the rule of seafood with white wine; all three of us would much rather drink a good cabernet.

"I never understood why this place is rarely crowded," Casey said. "It's right in the heart of things, it's a weekend night, food is great, and look . . . empty tables."

There was a scattering of mid-evening diners. A family of four, a young couple across from us, two older couples laughing through appetizers, and a woman who looked like the older Joni Mitchell sitting alone in a booth, sipping white wine.

"I don't mind the quiet," I said.

We had hoped to hike in the mountains during our time in Seattle, so we talked about some possible trails, made plans to see Pike Place Market and watch the vendors toss fish. I wanted Leslie to see some of the neighborhoods and, if the weather cleared, catch Mt. Rainier looming in the distance, like a nature god watching over the city.

"It looks like it's *right there*," said Casey, "but of course it is, what? Some sixty miles away?"

"You've found a home here, haven't you," Leslie asked.

It was an interesting question. Home?

"It's a good place," he said, pouring more wine.

It was wonderful to hear him say that. I knew it instinctively, I think, but when he said it out loud that night it seemed to solidify the reality. There had been health issues, a chronic illness that inflamed his cartilage indiscriminately; an autoimmune disorder that could strike without warning. Undetected, it could have killed him. It did damage his esophagus and the cartilage in his nose, but he was okay, alive, lucky. It was uncovered in his teenage years, and that helped. But that also was a curse; an unexpected demon he had to wrestle with at an age that already carried heavy burdens.

"I've always said I think the illness made me a better person," Casey said. He had learned to be at ease talking about it.

"I know exactly how you feel," said Leslie.

"Cancer survivor," I said.

Casey's eyes brightened.

The cancer had attacked Leslie's thyroid, there was a tumor on the spine, and a troubling early diagnosis. For Casey, an unknown ailment, pain and discomfort around cartilage in his nose and ears, the concerns for the cartilage in his heart, and an unexpected diagnosis of a rare chronic disease. Both of them had to fight off the possibility of death.

"I've come to find beauty in what happened to me," Leslie said, tasting her wine. "I could either take pity on myself or step up to the challenge."

"That's exactly it," Casey said. "My disease made me stronger, a better person. We are given only what we can handle. It was just time to go on living my life."

"So much is about attitude," Leslie said. "I am convinced."

If you had heard this exchange on a television show or a radio news program about survivors of medical conditions, you would have found it terribly predictable—two stories of perseverance and the power of will. But to me it was far beyond this. Nothing could have been more real, truer, more necessary than what these two were saying at that moment. And nothing could have been more outside my experience than what these two had been through. I had never faced death so directly. Yes, I had the minor heart attack a couple of years ago, but for me, that had far less weight than the heavy tests of human resolve that these two had confronted. Casey was my hero. Leslie was my heroine. I felt small in their presence, content to be lost in their shadows. I leaned back in my chair and drank my wine and listened as they talked of doctor appointments, mental strength, learned tenacity, and the benefits of what they had been given. My chest warmed; there was a tender rush of blood rising in my neck to my cheeks and my eyes. I swallowed hard and turned my head away from them as they talked, seeing the late-day sunlight reflect off the leftover streaks of rainwater on the restaurant's windows near the street.

Leslie excused herself to go to the restroom. Casey and I were alone, and again there was the desire to disclose the plan to move in with Leslie this summer. But I hesitated. Instead, I lifted my wineglass, and toasted to the upcoming one-year anniversary of Casey's move to Seattle. The two of us took long, deep drinks.

Chapter 18

Two oranges and a mango had been left on the kitchen counter; the blueberries had been left in the refrigerator to chill. I found a reasonably sharp knife in a drawer and began trimming the skin from the mango, being careful not to cut too deeply into the yellowish fruit. It's a bit tricky with a mango; the skin adheres to the fruit like aged Scotch tape left on a window. I placed slices of mango on the wooden cutting board and began to tear skin from one of the oranges, the fruit's distinct perfume filling the kitchen. A tug was needed to pull away the individual wedges. I placed each one on a colorful plate—a serving dish of blue and green found in the cupboard next to the refrigerator—and fanned out the mango slices like a dealer might display a deck of cards before a gambler. I rinsed the blueberries under the sink's faucet, picking away small stems and ill-formed berries from the batch and tossing in the garbage disposal. From my open palm, a handful of berries spilled to the plate and surrounded the pieces of mango and orange. I placed the dish in the center of the kitchen table, filled a kettle with water for coffee, and turned on the electric stovetop to boil water. Birds lightly chirped in a whisper near the west window that framed a morning of clouds and sun, a beautiful in-between.

Leslie was still inventing the night's final dreams, so I sat at the rectangular kitchen table near the window alone in the silvery gray of the early hours, letting everything wrap around me like an old quilt, the arms of solitude embracing me. On the small bookshelf in the kitchen was a copy of *Roget's Thesaurus*, a Spanish dictionary, *The Complete Guide to Gardening*, two editions of *The Joy of Cooking*, and a book entitled *Walls*. It was a sketchbook with each page depicting a brick wall, a wooden fence, or a stone doorway, inviting you to create your own graffiti—to draw or doodle. One houseguest had drawn a cartoon rock guitarist with a beard and long hair, angels swirled around him, and had written below: *'Scuse Me While I Kiss the Sky*. On the image of a gray stone wall I drew a coffee mug, an Underwood typewriter, flowers in a vase, a fish, and an acoustic guitar. I read from a book of poetry—*Aux Arcs* by Shin Yu Pai—with verses on apples, persimmon, and Tiananmen Square. Beside it on the shelf, a book as far from Chinese poetry as one can get, a cookbook—*Are You Hungry Tonight?: Elvis' Favorite Recipes*. Included were culinary instructions for black-eyed peas, collard greens, and many kinds of pies. Oddly enough, there was nothing on how to make a peanut butter and banana sandwich. Brenda Arlene Butler wrote the book. She was a self-proclaimed Elvis fan.

I poured ground coffee into a French press, added the hot water from the kettle, and sat the press on the table next to the plate of fruit. I toasted a wheat English muffin and spread a thin layer of marmalade on it. After four or five minutes, I plugged the press and poured the coffee in a white mug, leaned against the window and sipped. It was somewhere around seven in the morning, but I was only guessing. I had not looked at the time since rising. There was no need. Time was unnecessary. Nothing now was being measured in minutes; only by events, by experiences—the drive to Virginia, the performance there, the song I had written, the new ones I was trying to complete, the concert in Portland, the dinner with Leslie's friend, the train ride to Seattle, Leslie meeting Casey, last night's dinner. Music, places, people.

I finished the muffin, ate two slices of mango, tossed back the last of my coffee, and walked the narrow stairs to the second floor.

Leslie's bare shoulders peeked out from the top of the sheets; strands of hair fell across the white pillowcase. I crawled in beside her.

"Hi," she whispered, stretching an arm across my side.

I kissed her head. "Hi," I whispered back.

"I really like Casey," she said, her voice still full of sleep. She snuggled tight against me. "He's engaging."

I pulled her close, using the physical gesture as a way to thank her, affirm her assessment of my son. "You sleep all right?" I asked.

"He's not quiet," Leslie said, still talking about Casey. She turned her head toward me while continuing to rest it on the pillow.

"I didn't mean he was a mute," I said. "He can sometimes be reserved."

"He wasn't that at all."

"He felt comfortable, I'm sure."

There was a ding from Leslie's phone.

"Client. Geez," she said, rolling her eyes.

Leslie had hoped to complete a real estate transaction with new clients before the trip, but it didn't work out that way. She had been in touch with them several times since leaving Chicago. She knew she had to, but she also didn't want to.

"I'm going to have to check some email at some point," she said.

I smiled. "We're in no rush."

Leslie rested her body on her elbows and pulled herself up on the bed toward the headboard. "I'm realizing I'm not who I was in Iowa. I'm not living what I practiced."

The Iowa City move had been such an awakening for Leslie, fueling a new approach to life. But the return to Chicago had infused a forgotten level of anxiety she thought she had been able to wipe away. It had crept back like a viney weed in a garden.

"What you need is coffee, blueberries, and some mango," I said, stepping out of bed, and bowing like a royal servant. "Breakfast is served, my lady."

"Sounds perfect," she grinned.

I wasn't going to remind her that even though there's good energy, like real love, we are never truly everything we once were. It's that you-can't-go-home-again phenomenon. But she already knew that.

Leslie stepped out of the sheets.

"Thought anymore about Pittsburgh?" she asked.

I stood at the bedroom door, leaning on the jamb.

"I have to go," I said.

"You want me?"

"I would like that."

Leslie pulled her oversized Miami University sweatshirt over her head and pulled it down across her waist.

"Why do you think you need this?" she asked.

I had thought long about that. But it wasn't as complicated as the length of time considering it would have suggested.

"Time is unforgiving," I said. "I just think they deserve some more time to be formally remembered. Does that sound right?"

"And you feel like you're getting old, time is running out?" Leslie asked. "You're not old, you know?"

"Like I said, time is unforgiving."

I headed down the stairs to the kitchen to turn on the stove and boil more water in the kettle.

* * *

We spent the late morning in Ballard—Bauhaus coffee on Market, art and clothes shops on Leary. A misty rain fell, just enough to remind us we were in the Northwest, but not enough to have to duck away somewhere. Pike Place Market was next. "Touristy, kind of. But you just got to see it," I told Leslie. "It's actually a real working market. All the fish throwing is a bit of a show, though." We tasted salmon and walked through the artists' section. Leslie bought a hand purse.

"Here we go," I said. In the middle of the market you could see a small group gathering in front of a chest-high glass counter. "Toss time."

We stood to the right of the crowd and waited.

"Tell it go, Tony!" a man, wearing a tight knit cap and a long apron stained in fish juice hollered from in front of the counter next to stacks of giant crab legs on ice and what I think was flounder. He pointed to another man, presumably Tony, who stood behind the counter about twenty feet away. He held a large whole salmon, nearly twice as long as his arm and as big around as one's thigh. "Don't drop it," Tony demanded. The crowd laughed. A third man appeared from the back room, said nothing, and took his place in this fish-throwing triangle. "Wooh!" Tony yelled, hurling the big fish through the air to the man in the cap. He flung it to the third. And around it went, back and forth, to the applause of the crowd, each man giving the fish his signature spin or twist as he lobbed it.

"Let's find the gum wall," I said.

Leslie laughed.

I had mentioned the gum wall several times to Leslie. I'm sure she thought it was an odd obsession. Maybe it was. The wall is on Post Alley underneath the market. It's a brick alleyway covered with used chewing gum, every color you can imagine, some of it several inches deep, stretched and stuck into shapes and even words. The gum wall is about fifty feet long and some twenty feet high. People must have climbed on others shoulders to get up to the tallest point. A local theater in the alley once had a problem with patrons sticking their gum on the wall, even with the sign that read: PLEASE DON'T PUT YOUR GUM ON THE WALL. Every weekend, the stage crew would spend hours scraping it off. In time, they gave up. I liked the wall and the story behind it because, in its own way, the wall was a testament to a minor act of anarchy, a monument to thumbing your nose at authority.

"I love this place," I said, standing on one side of the alley to take a photograph.

"You would," Leslie said.

"Test authority," I said sternly.

"It's just a wall full of gum, babe."

"Oh, come on. It's more than that!"

Wonder if anyone has written a song about the gum wall? I thought.

* * *

We picked up Casey from the street corner near his office downtown and fought our way through one-way streets and heavy rush hour traffic back to Ballard, ordered Thai food to go, bought a bottle of red wine, and headed for the cottage to feast and drink at the kitchen table.

"So, you did the touristy stuff," Casey said, using a big spoon to dish out rice and pad thai into an oversized serving bowl. "Got to do it."

"It was fun," Leslie said. "Never been to Seattle, so."

"Hike tomorrow," I said.

"Not going to be able to get away," Casey said. "Just too much going on at work." He had video to edit and a project to complete.

"No worries. We'll meet you afterward," I said.

"Rattlesnake?" Casey asked.

"Yeah, if you think that's a decent day hike," I said.

The Rattlesnake Ridge hike was four miles in total near North Bend in the Cascades, about an hour outside Seattle. It had a pretty steep elevation change going up, but coming down was easier.

"Got to get to the top," Casey said. "Great view over this ledge that juts out. Even if it's foggy and rainy, it's worth it."

"Take Cody?" Leslie asked.

"That'd be great," Casey said. "He's good on a hike."

Leslie passed a dish of some other kind of noodle, something spicy.

"I'm good," Casey said.

"Is it killer hot?" I asked.

"Not killer," she said.

Casey took a sip of his wine. "So what's the owner like?" he asked.

I pointed out the wire artwork on the kitchen wall, the thousands of wick holders in the basket near the door, and the room where she worked during the day. "She has pieces in a gallery in Ballard," I said. "We walked by it today. What was it?" I asked Leslie. "Wasn't there something for $500?"

Leslie nodded. "Nice lady. She must do well."

"Older woman," I added.

Why I felt I needed to say that, I wasn't sure.

"Did I tell you we saw Dylan?" I asked Casey.

"Speaking of old," he said, slurping a noodle.

"It was really good," I said. "He gravels his way through the songs these days. Doesn't play guitar. Heard he has arthritis. But it's Dylan, you know?"

"I'd never seen him," Leslie said. "Now I can say I have."

"Got to see Dylan," I said.

It was my third time. I attended a concert alone inside a gymnasium at a small college outside Chicago sometime in the 1990s, if I remember correctly. And I saw him again with Willie Nelson outside at a minor league ballpark. I was still married then. We took the boys.

"I remember that concert," Casey said. "First time I smelled dope and saw people smoking it."

"You guys were pretty young," I said.

"Nice parental move, Dad," Casey joked.

"Dylan and Willie. Weed is going to be everywhere. Hard to avoid," I said. "You got over it."

"Does Graham remember any of it?" Leslie asked.

"Oh, yeah. He's told me," I said.

"Didn't you try to teach us the words to some song?" Casey asked.

"Stuck in Mobile with the Memphis Blues Again," I sang.

"Who sings that?" Casey asked sarcastically.

"Dylan!"

"Let's keep it that way," he teased.

"I hear a lot of this," Leslie said.

I rolled my eyes.

"Okay, okay. Dad likes Bob," I said.

I poured what was left of the wine, measuring out each glass to make it fair. We clinked the three of them to honor a good night and packed up the leftovers for Casey to take to his place. Leslie placed the now empty restaurant food containers in a bag and began gathering the dirty dishes.

"I got this," I said.

"No worries," Leslie said, continuing to clean up.

I stood from the table, "I can do this after Casey leaves. Don't worry about it, Marie."

"Whoa!" Casey blurted.

"What the fuck?" Leslie cried.

Both of them stood still and stared at me.

"Oh, shit," I groaned. "Where did that come from?"

"What the fuck?" Leslie asked again.

Casey smiled nervously. "Seriously, Dad?"

I threw my arms around Leslie. "Oh, I am so sorry, babe. Jesus. Really. I am so sorry." I tried to hold her tight. She did not hug back, her arms at her sides.

"Really?" Leslie sighed, grinning awkwardly, her face red with anger or embarrassment or both.

"And there you have it," Casey giggled, trying to lighten things up. "I think it's time for me to go."

"Babe, seriously, I'm so, so sorry. I don't understand what that was about," I said, now holding her hand.

"Just don't say that in bed," Leslie said, still grinning.

"Geez," I grunted.

There was an odd silence for just a moment, but it seemed like many minutes.

"It's okay," Leslie said. "You probably just felt comfortable with Casey here. All of us talking and everything. Like old times or something."

"Geez. I've been divorced for a long time."

Each of us had been knocked off balance, like a sailboat hit with a stormy gust. We collectively exhaled and steadied ourselves.

"Well, I guess I'll see you guys tomorrow night after the hike," said Casey, as we all walked toward the front door.

"We'll ring you when we're back and settled in," I said.

"We'll pick you up, I guess, right?" Leslie asked.

"Okay then. Goodnight, Dad," he said. "And goodnight . . . Marie."

All of us laughed. There was nothing else to do.

* * *

I was crushed, embarrassed, and empty. After Casey left, I couldn't say another word. I pulled deeply inward. Leslie told me again it was okay, but it wasn't. She headed upstairs to get ready for bed and I sat in the kitchen alone, silent and sullen. Later, I crawled into bed next to Leslie, trying not to touch, saying nothing, pretending to check emails on my phone. She attempted to engage, asking about the next day's hike plans, and commenting on the evening with Casey. But I was reticent, communicating with single words. She turned her body away from me and fell asleep while I stared at the shadow the street-light had cast on the wall. An hour later I was lying on the couch downstairs, staring at a different shadow. It was another hour before I fell asleep. At 4:00 am, I was awakened by a text on my phone. *Why aren't you sleeping with me?* I read the words three times then turned and buried my head in the couch's cushion. I was in and out of sleep until light entered through the window of the cottage's front door.

"What are you doing here?" Leslie said softly, stepping lightly across the hardwood floor from the stairway to the small living room and couch where I was curled up, motionless but awake under a heavy throw. "Why'd you sleep here?" She knelt beside the couch and touched my arm.

"Restless," I said. It was only partly true.

"Sorry," she said.

I closed my eyes. I could sense Leslie still at my side, but then she was gone.

Leslie put water on the stove for coffee. When the whistle sounded, I rose slowly, reluctantly. I used the bathroom, washed my hands, and placed my forehead against the mirror above the sink. My eyes were glassy. The lines in the corners appeared deeper than I had remembered.

Leslie stood at the kitchen window. She had placed the container of coffee grounds and the French press on the table. "I'm going to let you do this," she said, smiling. "You're the expert."

"I let you down," I said, placing my arms around her waist. "I really did."

"Is this about last night?"

"I feel worthless."

Leslie took my hands and held them to her chest. "I think you're having a harder time with this than me."

I was not the person I was when I married Marie. Leslie was not the person she was when she was married. She was not who she was before Iowa or after. And I was not who I was five, two, even one year ago. We never are. We never can be. We never should be. But we carry with us everything we once had been. It's stored away in the endless boxes, tucked away in the mind's attic. All of it is there—Christmas mornings, first dates, concerts, song lyrics and melodies. There is long-ago heartache, sorrow, joy, and love. None of it evaporates; it just takes on another form. Ice to water to vapor.

Chapter 19

Leslie and I hiked Rattlesnake Ridge for four hours. The two-mile uphill climb ended at a stony plateau that jutted into the fog far above the pines. Other hikers ventured close to the edge, but we chose to stay back several feet. The decision did not diminish the experience. The view was mystical. The walk back down took less time but required some caution. Occasional misty rain had produced a slippery trail, and when we reached the bottom, there was mud on our boots and Cody was half-covered, like a strawberry dipped in chocolate. It was all the way up his legs, inside the pads of his paws, on his tail, and across his chest, but not his neck, shoulders or face. We found a crank water fountain near the trailhead and I washed him down as best I could. There was an old University of Missouri blanket in the payload section of Casey's car and I used it to pat the dog dry, but not before Cody shook the excess bathwater off his coat and all over my legs. He was still a wet dog after the cleanup and that made the car smell like the inside of a damp, old barn.

A quiet nine-hole golf course sat in a valley a few miles from the trail entrance. We had passed it on the way up the mountain, noting the small wood frame clubhouse had a restaurant. The sign outside promoted its burgers. It looked like a good place for food after the hike. Cody could rest in the car with the back window rolled halfway down. The parking lot was nearly empty when I drove in, wind-burned and leg-tired from the hike.

"That was just right," Leslie said, sitting at a large table near the clubhouse's picture window that looked out toward the course. A man and a boy—likely a father and his son—were putting on the nearest green. Light rain fell.

"Good exertion," I said. "Could have done without the company."

"Forgot it was spring break," Leslie said.

The trail was more crowded than we would have thought or liked. College kids in groups—girls and guys, some playing music from their phones' speakers for all the wilderness to hear.

"Certainly have nothing against music, but why play it in the middle of the woods?" I wondered.

"You sound like a cranky old man," Leslie teased.

"Get off my lawn, you kids!" I growled, imitating a grumpy neighbor. "Yeah, I guess. But it just seemed, I don't know, out of place. There's a reverence in the woods."

"I agree. But not all of us think like that," Leslie reminded me.

We ordered French onion soup. I chose the roasted vegetable wrap. Leslie decided on a burger. It took a while for the food to arrive. No one working there was in any kind of a hurry.

"You should go out with Casey tonight. Just the two of you," Leslie suggested.

"Well, we could grab a bite and—"

"I'm not going to be hungry after this. Not right away," she interrupted. "You need to be with him and just hang out."

"I appreciate that. We could go to his favorite bar."

"Did you tell him yet?" she asked.

"Wanted to. Not yet. Tonight."

"You don't have to say anything just because of me, you know?"

"No. I'm going to. It's important."

"Don't turn it into some big thing, though."

"He should know and not hear it from his brother or his mother. It should come from me, face-to-face. Not over the phone or some text or something."

Leslie turned to the window and the green mountains. She appeared to be thinking. "Looks like it stopped raining."

"Rain or not, it's been quite nice."

"I think I need more sun," she said. "This is great. The mountains. Seattle, I think, is a cool part of the world. Our kind of town, right? But the weather?"

"It isn't always like this," I said. "Casey said this is more rain than they've had in some time."

"Well, what do they say?" she asked. "It's not the rain. It's learning to dance in it. Something like that, right?"

I smiled and said, "I don't think I could dance right now."

"Not sure I could *get up* right now," Leslie said.

A pleasant pain, a welcome ache had anchored us to the chairs. No matter, we had no place better to be.

* * *

Leslie sat at the kitchen table, skimming Facebook and occasionally checking her email. She was still wrestling with the clients back in Chicago. We had both showered and taken short naps. She relaxed. I dressed, checked for cash in my wallet, and tucked my phone in the front pocket of my jeans.

"You want me to bring back some food?" I asked.

"Maybe," she said. "I'll pull up the menu on the website and text you."

I kissed her on the forehead.

"Sure you don't want to come?"

"Go," she said. "This is good."

Percy's was a few blocks away. I met Casey at the corner and we walked together.

Local legend says Ballard at the turn of the nineteenth century had more bars than any other town west of the Mississippi River. Probably had something to do with all of the longshoremen or commercial fishermen. Percy Sankey had a tavern he named The Ballard Bar. He closed it during prohibition, sort of. The front door sign read PERCY'S MEN'S FURNISHING. But in the back, near the alley, was a secret entrance. That's where you'd find the bar. Nearly one hundred years later, Percy's—now called Percy's & Company—was still serving.

"Tell me about this one. The Blood and Sand," I asked the

bartender.

The drinks all had a twist to them, something new or different, a new take on an old concoction. At least that's what I thought.

"It has Scotch. Basically it's an old-fashioned," he said.

The waiter wasn't exactly selling it. I learned later the drink was named for the Rudolph Valentino movie, *Blood and Sand,* a movie about bullfighting. The cocktail was blood red. It had been around since the 1930s—something old was new again.

Casey ordered a Maker's Mark old-fashioned.

"See the guy at the end of the bar?" Casey asked. "He's the restaurant video guy I was telling you about."

Casey was just beginning a project focusing on Ballard restaurants, like mini-episodes of some Food Network show. He was the creative side; the guy at the end of the bar was the salesman.

"How's that going?" I asked.

"It's *going,*" he said. "Just getting started. We'll see."

Casey was cautious about praising his work in its early stages. His response made me think about the song I was trying to complete. It too was in the early stages and I could have responded the same way to a question about its progress: It's *going.*

We ordered fried almonds with rosemary salt, something to munch on. The bartender placed the drinks on the table.

"So, how's Leslie?" Casey asked.

I wasn't expecting that—a simple straightforward, open-ended question.

"Good," I said, swallowing the first taste of the Blood and Sand. "Real good." It was an opening to tell him about the two of us moving in together, but for some reason I didn't take it. "We get along so well, Casey."

"I can see that," he said.

"She loves my music. She loves animals. Our temperaments match." I was ready to tell him I was in love, but I think he knew that. "We have such good talks. I could talk to her forever."

"That's good for you, Dad."

"Here's a question for you. Leslie and I were talking about this the other day. What do pets actually feel? Emotionally, what are they capable of really feeling?"

"Sad, happy. The regular stuff," Casey said.

"Complex emotions?"

"What do you mean?"

"Leslie would say, 'Dakota's jealous.' Dakota's her dog."

"Okay"

"Jealous? Dogs can't feel jealousy."

"Why not? Maybe."

"I looked it up. Dogs—not cats—have the emotional capabilities of a two-year-old human."

"Can't a two-year-old feel jealous? That kid has something I got. I want one, too."

"Maybe that's not jealousy. That's just *I want.* Jealousy is more complicated."

"Okay."

"She'll say Dakota feels guilty. Dogs don't feel guilt."

"Don't two-year-olds feel some guilt? I think they do."

"Again, maybe not that complicated. Something like it, but not guilt."

"Hmmm. Okay. Guilt is complex."

Casey's glass had only ice remaining. I took the last sip of mine.

"Two more?" I asked.

"Oh yeah," Casey laughed.

Another Maker's Mark old-fashioned and Blood and Sand.

My phone buzzed. It was a text from Leslie. She'd decided on some food: *chicken liver mousse, baguette & pickles.* I texted back: *got it. may be awhile yet. u good?*

Take ur time, she responded. *Have fun.* Smiley face.

"Leslie?" Casey asked.

"Just going to order food for her to take back when we're

ready."

"No guilt?" Casey smiled.

I laughed. "No, no. It's you and me, my friend. It's cool."

Fresh drinks were placed on the table. We clinked the glasses and took long swallows.

"Guilt is a funny thing," I said. "Ever feel guilty?"

"Not really," Casey said, shaking his head. "Well, maybe."

"People can prod us into guilt. But we are the ones who allow it to happen, right? Did you ever feel guilty about moving so far away?"

Casey appeared puzzled. "You mean from home, Chicago?"

I nodded.

"Should I?" he asked, grinning.

"Of course not."

"*You* guilty about something, Dad?" he asked wryly.

"Oh, Jesus. You really want to get into that?"

"Oh, so you *are!*"

"No, no. Maybe feel bad about things at times, but not guilt. No."

"Guilt is ugly."

"Like you, I left home and moved to Chicago when I was young."

"Guilty about that?"

"One of the few times I remember seeing my father cry—the night before I packed up the truck to drive five hundred miles away."

"Pappy didn't seem like the crying type."

"When he buried our dog in the front lawn under the big pine and when I left for Chicago."

"And Nanny?" he asked.

"She didn't cry when I left. She was always stronger than Dad."

"But she felt it inside, I'm sure," Casey said.

Was I responsible for how my parents felt when I left? Was I responsible for a failed marriage? Partly, yes, but guilty? No. Was I always the best father? I'll take the blame for being short-tempered with my sons at times when they were kids, but was I guilty? No. Was I guilty for not spending more time with my father when he was dying? Certainly there is some regret for not seeing my mother more often when she was in her last months. But I did not have guilt. No. I am sure I could make a long list of reasons I could have allowed guilt to clamp onto me. But truly it is too strong a word to describe any of those experiences. Guilt is about compromising yourself, breaking some moral compass. And it doesn't even have to be real; accuracy is not a necessary element. So no. Not guilt.

"They're playing good music in here," I said.

"Is that Motown?"

"Not always a big Motown guy, but some songs are just, you know, fun."

"My Girl" played through the bar's speakers.

"And certainly after a couple of drinks," Casey said, raising his glass.

Now was the time to tell him.

"I just wanted to let you know," I said, swirling the ice around in the tumbler, the Temptations playing as my soundtrack, "in a couple of months, Leslie and I are moving in together."

"Okay," he said, matter-of-factly, as if already knowing.

"I didn't want to tell you over the phone, in a text or something."

"Sure."

"Wanted it face-to-face."

"I understand."

"I'm going to her place. Makes the best sense. She has a house."

"Yeah, sounds right."

"So, yeah. It's time."

"It's not that big a deal, Dad," he said. "I have friends who have moved in with their girlfriends."

It was a big deal. It was a big deal for me, for Leslie.

"We are really good together," I said.

"You're not getting married, right?"

"I don't know if I'll ever get married again, Casey. But, make no mistake. I don't take this lightly. It's a commitment."

"I live more than a thousand miles away," he said. "I guess that's what I mean about it not being a big deal. It just doesn't really mean a lot to me in my daily life, you know?"

I could tell he wasn't trying to diminish the news I was delivering, but he was right. It didn't truly matter in the daily scheme of his life.

"You're happy?" Casey asked.

"She is exactly what I need," I said.

Casey pointed to my glass. "Another?"

"Man, I don't know."

"Seriously? When do we get to do this sort of thing?" Casey waved to the bartender.

Another Marker's Mark old-fashioned; another Blood and Sand. We drank the last round in happy silence.

As we exited Percy's, "I Heard It Through the Grapevine" played over the tavern's speakers. I carried a small brown box—Percy's doggie bag—with an order of liver mousse in a tiny white ceramic container and French bread packaged in wax paper. Two pickles were wrapped separately. What remained of the Seattle night was crisp but not cold. No rain. I slapped Casey on the back as we walked out onto Ballard Avenue and toward Vernon Place.

"You know the words to that song?" I asked. "Come on, sing it with me."

"The grapevine song?" Casey chuckled.

"Marvin Gaye," I added. "Everyone knows this!"

"Didn't Credence or someone do a version?"

"Oh my, I brought you up right, didn't I?"

"Credence!" I yelled into the night.

Two hours ago, belting out a band's name like that might have been a little embarrassing, and singing, "I Heard it Through the Grapevine" out loud under Ballard streetlights would have been unlikely. But what might have been and all of what had come before no longer mattered. This night was meant to be exactly as it had turned out to be, a father and his son, loosened by liquor, singing Motown all the way back home.

Chapter 20

It was our last morning in Seattle. Leslie sat at the kitchen table, looking out the window at the flowers and the cottage's emerald green grass.

"I don't know exactly how I want my garden to look," she said, considering what to do with a triangular plot of land behind her house outside Chicago. "But I do know exactly how I want it to feel."

Earlier, I had watched Leslie get ready. I stood in the doorway to the bathroom as she combed her hair before the mirror and carefully chose the bracelets she wanted to wear. We talked and she dressed. Like the garden she would eventually plant at her new home, preparing herself for our last day in Seattle was less about how she wanted to look and more about how she hoped to feel. Her sparkling eyes and her throaty laugh were intoxicating and would draw any man close. But it was her connection to this kind of soulfulness that had hooked me from the start.

"I get that," I said, pouring coffee into a mug and taking a seat at the table across from Leslie.

"You don't want to overdo it," she said, looking out the window to the cottage's landscape. "I have a vision and I think a lot of what's out there is part of it. Little by little it will come together."

"That the kind of house you want when you retire?"

"A cottage. Wildflowers," she said, mocking my memory. "We talked about this."

There was a soft knock at the rear door. Patti, the house's owner, peeked inside. She had come to say goodbye.

We handed over the keys, double-checked if we emptied the trash and the recycling in the proper cans, and raved about the neighborhood, her artwork, and how well we slept in her studio home.

"It's a good place," Patti said. "Ballard used to be full of old Scandinavian ladies with lots of cats, but that was a long time ago. So much change."

Leslie and I walked the few blocks to Java Bean. Yelp suggested it was Ballard's best coffee shop, but I suspect Yelp had a lot of "best coffee shops" in Seattle. We had time to kill before the taxi would come to take us to the downtown train station and the airport.

"I don't think I was like Casey when I was younger." I said, sitting at a small round table over a skim latte.

"You mean to move so far from where he grew up?" Leslie asked.

"The physical distance isn't really the thing," I said. "I like to think I would have been that brave. But it's more about the distance in his head."

"He's far from the old home in Chicago, isn't he?"

"He's gone."

"But don't we all do that?"

"You hope you move on, change, grow."

"Oh sure, I'm still doing it. My time in Iowa, all of that."

"And it wasn't the physical distance."

"It wasn't anything about that, really. Not in the end," Leslie said.

"And when I move in with you, how does that all fit in?" I asked.

"More growth, right?" Leslie asked. "But you're not bringing a lot of stuff with you," she joked.

"Books, the dog, and my old guitar," I said, smiling. "It's all I need."

From time to time I've considered buying a travel guitar, one of those especially designed portable six strings that fits in the overhead compartment of an airplane. They're quite sleek and simple, some even fold up, but still process a pretty good sound. I thought it would be cool to have a six string that was easy to take on vacation or a work trip, an anytime-anywhere guitar that I could breakout whenever the spirit moved me. But I always talk myself out of it. I have a guitar.

"It would be nice to pick away on that old thing right now," I said, standing to get a refill on the coffee.

I bought my 1970s-era Yamaha acoustic with the dollars I had saved from delivering newspapers as a teenager. And now, decades later at Java Bean in Ballard, I longed for that guitar on my lap, one hand on the neck and the other free to strum. I so badly wanted to play. Not for Leslie, not for the patrons of that coffee shop. I only wanted to play for *me*. No matter what I had become, what I was or thought I'd be, I was always the guitar man. Not a virtuoso, not a master, but the guy with the wooden six string who since those long-haired high school days when he was intoxicated by the music of the times had turned the instrument into a vessel for every emotion he had ever experienced. Without the guitar, I was simply not myself. Not then, not now. It was and is my constant counselor, my life's single pillar. And now, with that guitar more than two thousand miles away, I missed it like an old friend.

"Inspired?" Leslie asked. "A song?"

"Always somehow," I said.

The taxi was on time; the train was fast. We ate fish and chips at the airport. And on the plane, somewhere over the Rocky Mountains, I lifted the middle arm between our coach seats and Leslie rested her head on my shoulder and we slept together the rest of the way to Chicago.

* * *

The plan was to be living together by mid-summer and I had been cleaning out closets and drawers to get ready. I had tossed out stacks of old bank statements, paperwork from two houses ago, sold a bunch of books. That was hard. I sold an end table, a set of shelves, and some cookware. And late one quiet night while clearing out a clothes closet, far in the back, I discovered a forgotten shoebox. Inside were audiotapes—several cassettes and small reel-to-reels. The reels were in thin square cardboard boxes, the cassettes in clear plastic cases. Hastily handwritten labels, now faded and tattered, were stuck to the cassettes. Black ink handwriting identified what was in the reel boxes. A few of the cassettes were mix tapes from the 1970s—songs from CSN&Y, the Allman Brothers, and Jackson Browne. Others were of a radio show I hosted on the campus station. Tucked at the very bottom was another set of tapes—two reel-to-reels and three cassettes— held tightly together in a single group with a thick rubber band. On the top was a white box holding a single five-inch reel-to-reel spool and written on the outside:

She's the One
Dave Berner

It was the recording of a song that I had written for my college girlfriend nearly forty years before, the one I almost married, the one who broke it off after seven years together. I performed it inside a radio station production studio in Pittsburgh sometime in the early 1980s, a few years after college graduation. I knew the production director at the time. We were able to sneak in late on a Saturday night when no one was around and lay down the song with an acoustic guitar—that old Yamaha—and two vocal tracks. I sang lead and harmony. I had tried to write a biting yet tender breakup song. Don't know if I succeeded, but I could still recall how good it felt to sing and capture it that night.

Along with it was another white square box, this one bigger and more frayed at the corners. On the outside it read:

The Bedroom Tapes

It was a direct riff off The Basement Tapes, Dylan's iconic recordings with The Band at his home in Woodstock. But, like the label suggested, the songs on this tape were recorded in a bedroom, my bedroom at my parents' house sometime around

1976. For four days, a high school buddy and I played guitars and sang before two microphones—over and over and over again— into a clunky reel-to-reel tape recorder that my mother and father had given to me for Christmas. No original songs that I remembered. Instead, we covered Stephen Stills' "Change Partners" and I'm sure something from America.

The faded writing on the worn labels on the other tapes in the stack—the three cassettes—suggested these were recordings of songs I had loved to sing and maybe something I had written back in my early twenties, a song recorded late at night in a smoky dorm room or disheveled college apartment, a composition I had long forgotten how to play. And now here I was, decades later, sitting on the floor of my apartment, holding each of the tapes in my hand, slowly running a finger over each label. I opened the reel boxes and held the plastic spools. I turned the cassettes over in my hand to study the front and back, as if examining old discarded photographs. I thought I might have known what had been captured on all that magnetic tape, but the only way I'd ever be certain would be to play them. I had no cassette player. I didn't even know where I could find one. A reel-to-reel machine would be even harder to secure.

I put the mix tapes and the recordings from the campus radio station back in the shoebox, placing it in the corner of my living room. I stacked the two reel-to-reels and the three cassettes together in a single group. As I tried to secure the old rubber band around them, it snapped. Age had weakened the rubber and it could no longer handle one more stretch. I searched for another on my desk, in kitchen drawers, and inside my toolbox. No rubber band. I had nothing to hold them together. I found a clear, clean plastic Ziploc bag in the kitchen—the kind used to store food—placed the tapes inside, secured the bag's seal, and placed the bag in the back of the top drawer of my dresser, next to a small hand Bible my grandmother had carried in her purse all her life and a yellow velour ring box containing my mother's diamond wedding ring and one of my father's old cufflinks.

Eventually, I would finish the song I had been writing for Leslie, and we would take that road trip to Pittsburgh and stand before my parents' graves. I'd have another prostate test and it would be okay. And I would gather up all those newly found recordings, pack them away in a carefully labeled brown cardboard box, carry them with me to the home Leslie and I would now share, and tuck them away on a high shelf behind my shirts in a bedroom closet.

I would most likely never again listen to what was on those tapes, but I would always know exactly where to find them.

David W. Berner is the author of three memoirs and a work of fiction. He is a journalist, writer, and broadcaster, and teaches in the School of Media Arts at Columbia College Chicago. He was named the writer-in-residence at the Jack Kerouac Project of Orlando in 2013, and the writer-in-residence at the Ernest Hemingway Foundation of Oak Park, Illinois in 2016.

Roundfire

FICTION

Put simply, we publish great stories. Whether it's literary or
popular, a gentle tale or a pulsating thriller, the connecting
theme in all Roundfire fiction titles is that once you pick them
up you won't want to put them down.
If you have enjoyed this book, why not tell other readers by
posting a review on your preferred book site. Recent bestsellers
from Roundfire are:

The Bookseller's Sonnets
Andi Rosenthal

The Bookseller's Sonnets intertwines three love stories with a tale
of religious identity and mystery spanning five hundred years
and three countries.
Paperback: 978-1-84694-342-3 ebook: 978-184694-626-4

Birds of the Nile
An Egyptian Adventure
N.E. David

Ex-diplomat Michael Blake wanted a quiet birding trip up the
Nile – he wasn't expecting a revolution.
Paperback: 978-1-78279-158-4 ebook: 978-1-78279-157-7

Blood Profit$
The Lithium Conspiracy
J. Victor Tomaszek, James N. Patrick, Sr.

The blood of the many for the profits of the few... *Blood Profit$*
will take you into the cigar-smoke-filled room where American
policy and laws are really made.
Paperback: 978-1-78279-483-7 ebook: 978-1-78279-277-2

The Burden
A Family Saga
N.E. David

Frank will do anything to keep his mother and father apart. But
he's carrying baggage – and it might just weigh him down ...
Paperback: 978-1-78279-936-8 ebook: 978-1-78279-937-5

The Cause
Roderick Vincent

The second American Revolution will be a fire lit from an
internal spark.
Paperback: 978-1-78279-763-0 ebook: 978-1-78279-762-3

Don't Drink and Fly
The Story of Bernice O'Hanlon: Part One
Cathie Devitt

Bernice is a witch living in Glasgow. She loses her way in her
life and wanders off the beaten track looking for the garden of
enlightenment.
Paperback: 978-1-78279-016-7 ebook: 978-1-78279-015-0

Gag
Melissa Unger

One rainy afternoon in a Brooklyn diner, Peter Howland punctures an egg with his fork. Repulsed, Peter pushes the plate away and never eats again.
Paperback: 978-1-78279-564-3 ebook: 978-1-78279-563-6

The Master Yeshua
The Undiscovered Gospel of Joseph
Joyce Luck

Jesus is not who you think he is. The year is 75 CE. Joseph ben Jude is frail and ailing, but he has a prophecy to fulfil ...
Paperback: 978-1-78279-974-0 ebook: 978-1-78279-975-7

On the Far Side, There's a Boy
Paula Coston

Martine Haslett, a thirty-something 1980s woman, plays hard on the fringes of the London drag club scene until one night which prompts her to sign up to a charity. She writes to a young Sri Lankan boy, with consequences far and long.
Paperback: 978-1-78279-574-2 ebook: 978-1-78279-573-5

Tuareg
Alberto Vazquez-Figueroa

With over 5 million copies sold worldwide, *Tuareg* is a classic adventure story from best-selling author Alberto Vazquez-Figueroa, about honour, revenge and a clash of cultures.
Paperback: 978-1-84694-192-4

Readers of ebooks can buy or view any of these bestsellers by clicking on the live link in the title. Most titles are published in paperback and as an ebook. Paperbacks are available in traditional bookshops. Both print and ebook formats are available online.

Find more titles and sign up to our readers' newsletter at http://www.johnhuntpublishing.com/fiction

Follow us on Facebook at https://www.facebook.com/JHPfiction and Twitter at https://twitter.com/JHPFiction

Printed and bound by PG in the USA